SHORT CUTS

SCIENCE FICTION CINEMA

FROM OUTERSPACE TO CYBERSPACE

GEOFF KING AND TANYA KRZYWINSKA

WALLFLOWER

LONDON and NEW YORK

A Wallflower Paperback

First published in Great Britain in 2000, reprinted in 2002, 2006
Wallflower Press
6a Middleton Place, Langham Street, London W1W 7TE
www.wallflowerpress.co.uk

A catalogue record for this book is available from the British Library

ISBN 1 903364 03 5

Book design by Rob Bowden Design

Printed in Great Britain by Antony Rowe Ltd, Chippenham, Wiltshire

CONTENTS

LIST OF ILLUSTRATIONS

ACKNOWLEGEMENTS

The authors would like to thank Alan Miller for reading the manuscript, David Bessell for his advice on film music and sound and the students on our 'Science Fictions' module at Brunel University.

INTRODUCTION: SPECTACLE AND SPECULATION

Science fiction has become one of the most popular *genres** in the cinema. Once confined largely to the ranks of lowly B-movies, it has become the stuff of hundred-million-dollar budgets and massive special effects. It plays a major part in the landscape of contemporary film, especially in its dominant Hollywood incarnation. From lurid comic-book blockbusters to dark *dystopian** visions, science fiction dominates many of our movie screens and can be seen as a powerful cultural barometer of our times. Images that spring to mind when we think of science fiction cinema might include *Star Trek*'s Enterprise gliding through space towards uncharted planets in yet another sequel, a silver-suited Flash Gordon doing battle with the fiendish Ming the Merciless, or the shape-shifting special effects of *Terminator 2: Judgement Day* (1991). These have become powerful icons in films watched by millions, yet the genre also extends into a wider range of industrial, historical and cultural contexts.

Science fiction has deployed a wide variety of aesthetic styles, from the clunky realism of *Destination Moon* (1950) to the comic-book fantasy world of *Flash Gordon* and the mystical or intellectual explorations of *2001: A Space Odyssey* (1968) and *Solaris* (1972). Even in the most sublimely trashy examples, the lure of the genre lies at least partly in its capacity to open up imaginative possibilities. Through the 'magic' of special effects, science fiction creates new spaces, dimensions and frontiers that re-define the human sphere of operation and often challenge

---

* terms indicated with an asterisk throughout the book are defined in the Glossary

1

our definitions of what exactly it is to be human. From the expansiveness of deep space to the *fractal** world of digital landscapes, science fiction links visions of science and the unknown to speculations about human evolution and destiny.

Why exactly is science fiction so popular in the cinema? How do the pleasures offered to audiences accord with the commercial goals of the film industry? This book offers answers to these questions through an overview of the genre and by locating its forms, themes and concerns within their social and industrial contexts. We argue that science fiction deals with the problems and promises offered by science, technology and rationality in an imaginative context given shape by the aims of the film industry. Science fiction often draws upon concerns about the definition of the human, a subject explored through a characteristic play of binary oppositions such as alien/machine versus human. The cinema of science fiction, like others, can be read in terms of the issues with which it appears to engage: a thematic analysis, in other words, which seeks to draw out the possible implications of what is found in individual films or genres.

Various different theoretical perspectives can be used in the analysis of the dominant themes of science fiction cinema. Several are used, implicitly or explicitly, in this book. Much of the first section views the cinema of science fiction from the perspective of issues considered to be of importance to the society or societies in which it has been produced; both as an *expression* of social concerns – especially those revolving around issues of science, technology and rationality – and as part of a cultural process in which such concerns might also be *negotiated* to some extent. This kind of reading leads, inevitably, into areas of political and/or ideological analysis: the way sensitive or contentious issues are handled has political implications – radical, reactionary or a combination of the two. Issues of social-political concern, particularly those relating to gender, are also approached in some cases from a perspective informed by psychoanalytical theories that have loomed large in cinema studies in recent decades.

Much debate continues around the use of any or all of these perspectives. How legitimate is it to make great claims – social, political or psychoanalytical – for the form or contents of science fiction films? We all have our own agendas in this respect. The aim of this book is not to claim 'scientific' status for its arguments. It is to provide a survey of what appear to us to be some of the key thematic, formal and industrial characteristics of science fiction in the cinema. Some of this may be considered speculative – like science fiction itself – although efforts have been made to ground our arguments. Textual analysis is one major source of evidence; although, as we suggest, different and perhaps competing interpretations can often be made of the same textual material. Another is consideration of the industrial contexts within which science fiction has been produced. Examination of industrial context, especially that of contemporary Hollywood, can help to account for many its features. Social-cultural and industrial perspectives are sometimes divergent, providing different explanations for the same phenomena, but sometimes mutually reinforcing. Study of actual audience reactions is beyond the scope of this book, however (for an example of an audience study of a recent Hollywood science fiction film see Barker and Brooks 1998, on *Judge Dredd* (1995)).

Section 1 of *Science Fiction Cinema* examines the dominant themes that help to give science fiction its identity. Section 2 considers the industrial context, focused primarily on Hollywood, as well as dimensions such as special effects and production design. These approaches are then combined in a case study of *Star Wars: Episode I – The Phantom Menace* (1999)

From the 1890s to the current Hollywood romance with special effects extravaganzas, science fiction cinema has borrowed from a variety of sources. These range from Greek tragedy and the epic to melodrama and gothic fiction, from the western and horror novel to the literature of science fiction. It also exchanges ideas, forms and images with media as varied as comics, television, radio, video games, religion, philosophy and science itself. Science fiction plays on current controversies about technological innovations or scientific discoveries, which can provide a source of dramatic tension and contemporary relevance. *Intextextual links** supply science fiction with an abundant source of references that can give mythic resonance to topical interest. It is precisely science fiction's diversity and flexibility, through its ability to absorb ideas from other domains, that has kept the genre alive for more than a century.

Science fiction has recently enjoyed unprecedented success and popularity in the cinema. Prompted by the huge box-office earnings of *Star Wars* (1977), contemporary Hollywood has invested heavily in the development of special effects technologies used to produce big-budget and heavily marketed films such as *Independence Day* (1996), *Armageddon* (1998) and *The Phantom Menace*. This is in marked contrast to the status of science fiction in Hollywood in the 1950s. During this period – now often described as the 'classic' era – science fiction was largely produced in low-budget 'B' formats, designed for a predominantly teenage audience. Such films built on the success of science fiction as a popular literary form, particularly in magazines such as *Astounding Science Fiction* (1930–1996), *Weird Tales* (1923–1954) or EC comics. Despite the formulaic, sensationalist and gimmicky nature of some of these films, they played an important part in shaping the distinctive themes and forms of the genre. Many can be related to concerns about the cold war and/or nuclear weapons, including a large group labelled 'invasion narratives' (see Sontag 1966; Biskind 1983; Tudor 1989; Jancovich 1996). The decade saw Earth or humanity constantly threatened by aliens in films such as *The Thing* (1951), also known as *The Thing (From Another World)*, *War of the Worlds* (1953) and *Earth vs. the Flying Saucers* (1956). Alternatively, the danger comes from humanity's own creations, usually the bizarre offspring of radiation experiments, as in *The Beast From 20,000 Fathoms* (1953), *Them!* (1954) and *Gojira* (1954).

Another theme of 1950s science fiction is the suggestion that people are being 'substituted' or 'depersonalised' as a result of alien encounters, a phenomenon explored in *It Came From Outer Space* (1953), *Invasion of the Body Snatchers* (1956) and *The Brain Eaters* (1958). The 'meaning' of these films offers a good example of the different interpretations that can sometimes be made of popular science fiction. Most obviously, these films can be taken as a displaced comment on the nature of the supposed threat

FIGURE 1 *Flash Gordon (1936)*

represented by the 'inhuman' regimentation of communism. At the same time, however, the idea that people might be 'taken over' in this brain-numbing manner has been related to concerns much closer to home: the fear expressed by some sociologists that 1950s America was sinking into a morass of suburban conformity and complacency. Traces of these films appear in later works as diverse as *Village of the Damned* (1960), *The Stepford Wives* (1975) and *Videodrome* (1982). Some 1950s films, such as *The Day the Earth Stood Still* (1951), presented themselves as more 'serious' and 'respectable' than the routine drive-in fodder. But many of the low-budget, comic-book-style films of the decade are now regarded as camp or trash classics. Examples such as *Plan 9 From Outer Space* (1958) and *Queen of Outer Space* (1958) are celebrated for their low quality and exaggerated depiction of gender. Others are fondly remembered for their use of quirky new technologies such as 3D.

The 1950s play a pivotal role in the history of popular science fiction cinema, looking back to serials of the 1930s such as *Flash Gordon*, and also taken as a key point of reference for the contemporary Hollywood blockbuster. The 1950s theme of depersonalisation has been played for comic value as far back as the short 'tricks' films of the early cinema, including George Méliès' films about automata, *Gugusse et l'Automate* (1897) and the now lost *Coppélia ou la Poupée Animée* (1900); the theme is also central to Fritz Lang's bleak vision of the future in *Metropolis* (1927).

What all these films have in common is that they deploy the special effects of their day to create a sense of unfamiliarity and spectacle. The gadgetry and exploitation aspects of 1950s films proved durable and still attract audiences on television and video. A very different strain of films was influenced by the intellectual aspirations of the European 'art' cinema of the 1950s and 1960s, often working outside Hollywood or in the independent sector. Films such as *2001: A Space Odyssey*, *Solaris*, *La Jetée* (1963), *Alphaville* (1965) and *Born in Flames* (1983) use science fiction to explore existential and/or political questions that were implicit in some of the films of the 1950s. The late 1970s saw the emergence of blockbuster science fiction films that sought and often achieved a much wider audience. *Star Wars* and *E.T. The Extra-Terrestrial* (1982) topped the box-office charts partly by targeting children and the 'family' audience. The science fiction blockbuster often uses the sale of branded merchandise to increase its revenues and as a form of marketing for the films themselves. The science fiction of recent blockbusters has demonstrated a number of strategies, including homage to the 1950s in *Mars Attacks!* (1996) and to the 1960s television serial in *Lost in Space* (1998). It has also maintained strong links with the disaster movie – *Armageddon* (1988), *Deep Impact* (1998) – and the horror film – the *Alien* quartet (1979, 1986, 1992, 1997), *Event Horizon* (1997) and *Cube* (1997).

It would be a mistake to think of science fiction cinema as solely a Hollywood phenomenon. During the past hundred years or so science fiction themes have been tackled in diverse ways, using different aesthetic strategies in varying national and industrial contexts. Space, science and technology have provided productive catalysts for the imagination of both big-budget and independent science fiction film-makers. Nevertheless, the wealth and global reach of Hollywood has ensured its domination and its capability to set industrial standards in certain aspects of the genre such as the quality of special effects.

Spectacle and *speculation* sum up two key dimensions of the genre. In imaginatively figuring the future (or an alternative past or present) science fiction films can be seen to some extent as measures of the hopes and fears of the cultures in which the films are produced and consumed. Science fiction plays a part in shaping the ways technology impacts on our lives; often selling or showcasing technologies, either as an expanded form of *product placement** or through the special effects deployed to tell the story. The imaginary work of science fiction might also open up horizons in the development of 'real' science. Popular interest in *virtual reality** technologies has been fuelled by films such as *The Lawnmower Man* (1992), *Strange Days* (1995), *eXistenZ* (1999) and *The Matrix* (1999). Films such as *Armageddon* and *Apollo 13* (1995) play a part in the promotion of the massive spending involved in the American space programme (see Penley 1997). Scientists may criticise the way their work is depicted in science fiction but this provides further confirmation of the role the genre can play in popular understandings of science and technology. Whatever its precise meanings or impact, science fiction has gone from humble and diverse beginnings to its current position as one of the most popular and lucrative genres in cinema history.

1   DEFINING SCIENCE FICTION: NARRATIVE THEMES

Science Fiction as a Genre

What makes science fiction a distinct genre? Most of us can probably recognise an example of science fiction when we see it. But what are the terms in which this genre is identified? What *exactly* makes a film science fiction? Is it the setting, the characters, the look of the film or the kinds of plots and themes that are explored? One useful way to open up this question is the distinction made by Rick Altman (1984) between *semantic** and *syntactic** ways of understanding genre – an approach taken from the study of language that provides a helpful analytical tool.

A semantic approach focuses on the units of meaning: the various different elements that make up a film or a genre. These units of meaning include things like the setting, for example. So, a science fiction film might be defined partly in terms of a semantic feature such as a setting in the future or in another galaxy or dimension. Other semantic elements include objects such as spaceships and the products of new technologies. Particular types of characters are also found, including scientists, cyborgs and aliens. Some semantic features are more specific to the medium of film. Science fiction cinema might be defined in terms of a certain visual style or by the use of flashy special effects. This semantic approach is useful and probably not far from the way we identify genres in everyday viewing. However, there are limits to how far it takes us. Listing the elements that identify a film with a particular genre is a *descriptive* approach. It tells us what kinds of elements are present, but does not say much about how they are used, what their effect might be or how their meaning might change over time. If we want to go further, to *analyse* what these films are doing, it needs to be combined with a syntactic approach.

In the study of language, the semantic dimension focuses on the meaning of individual words. Syntax is the grammatical structure into which these words are organised. A syntactic approach to genre, then, examines how the different elements of meaning are organised. A genre defined in this way does not depend merely on the existence of the required elements, but on the organisation of these elements into recurring and familiar patterns. Much of the first section of this book will be an examination of some of the thematic patterns into which the various elements of science fiction films are organised; or, at least, narrative patterns that are available to be 'read into' them, often independently of authorial intent, and that might be subject to debate.

The combination of semantic and syntactic approaches recommended by Altman can provide a way of understanding the historical development of genres and how they might undergo subsequent change. A genre might exist in its early stage only in semantic terms – a few familiar elements – and only gradually develop a stable and reworked syntax. Alternatively, there might be cases in which the syntax stays the same but some of the semantic elements change. This is one way of understanding the claim that a film like *Star Wars* is 'really' a western: key semantic elements have changed (space and spacecraft replace the west and men on horseback), but the patterns into which they are arranged have much in common. A combination of the semantic and syntactic approaches offers a way of exploring genres that is especially useful in the analysis of Hollywood, where many genre boundaries are often blurred. It helps to draw attention to the flexible qualities of genres. This is more helpful than attempting to draw up rigid boundaries between one genre and another. Hollywood has always tended to mix components from different genres, in an attempt to repeat or play off past commercial success and to appeal to different sections of the audience (for the best recent work on these aspects of genre in Hollywood see Altman 1999 and Neale 2000).

Science fiction, like all genres, is a 'leaky' and relatively unstable category that borrows from and informs other genres. Like Frankenstein's creature, it is a hybrid, the body of which is comprised of parts of other discourses and texts. A number of recent Hollywood blockbusters might be defined as science fiction, for example, but also as a somewhat fuzzy mixture of science fiction and action-adventure, often with doses of disaster, romance and comedy thrown in for good measure. We might talk about some kind of 'gravitational pull' around certain core themes and styles, but these are always open to negotiation and change. As a genre, science fiction needs to add new twists to its conventions and to react to cultural and technological change if audience interest is to be maintained. At the same time, some key themes and images have proved remarkably resilient. One genre relationship that has troubled many critics – between science fiction and horror – will be explored later in this section of the book.

Humanity versus Science, Technology and Rationality

How are the various elements of science fiction films organised? How can we move from a semantic to a syntactic analysis of the genre, from listing characteristic elements to an analysis of the relationships into which they are patterned? The different elements of films or genres can be read in terms of patterns of *oppositions* between different elements. One key opposition found in science fiction films is between the 'human' and the products of *science**, *technology** and *rationality**. The elements of a science fiction film might be lined up on one side of this opposition or the other. The central figure is likely to be representative of the human. Other elements, including aliens, computers and cyborgs, might represent an alternative of one kind or another, although science fiction is often at its most interesting when the lines become blurred.

Many science fiction films can be read as explorations of the fate of humanity in a world often depicted as increasingly dominated by the

11

products of science, technology and rationality. Humans are supposed to embody particular qualities – especially feelings, intuition and emotions – that often clash with the demands of 'scientific' objectivity or rationality. Science fiction films can be seen as an arena in which we can explore exactly what it is to be 'human', partly through the juxtaposition between the human and a variety of opposites that will be explored in more detail below.

This way of reading science fiction films owes much to a *structuralist** approach to cultural products pioneered by the French social anthropologist Claude Lévi-Strauss (1968). A structuralist analysis views cultural products, such as myths or popular films, as devices through which societies try to work out difficult issues in one way or another, directly or implicitly. What these products appear to offer in many cases is an imaginary way of resolving problems that may be impossible to resolve in reality. They take on board very real difficulties and give the appearance of bringing about a 'magical' resolution (for a standard reading of genre in these terms, but one that does not include science fiction, see Schatz 1981; for a critique, see Neale 1999). Many science fiction films can be read as offering this kind of imaginary resolution of the opposition between the human and science, technology and rationality. They often set up an initial opposition that is eventually reconciled. Real issues are raised and difficulties are sometimes tackled quite seriously, but in mainstream films they are more likely to be evaded in the pursuit of a more reassuring narrative closure.

This is one area in which readings in terms of social-cultural context can be integrated with, or challenged by, considerations of industrial strategy. The reconciliation of difficult issues might serve a cultural purpose, in the terms suggested by Levi-Strauss or Schatz, but it is also a potential source of pleasure for the viewer. A working through and removal of anxieties that are present in the broader cultural context – as fears of technology are in ours, a subject of frequent media debate and 'scare' stories – offers, potentially at least, the kind of pleasurable release that might contribute to success at the box office. Social-cultural and industrial explanations can be mutually reinforcing, but not always.

A specific focus on the industrial dimension can also provide some protection against the temptation to make too many generalised assumptions about the cultural 'meaning' of popular films. Neither science fiction films nor any others 'plug in', immediately, to social concerns. Such concerns, as far as they are manifested in the cinema, are mediated through commercial/industrial imperatives. An upsurge or decline in production within a particular genre, such as science fiction, might be attributed to changes in the social and historical background; but it might equally be explained by shifting industrial strategies.

Rational Dreams and Technological Nightmares: Utopia and Dystopia in Science Fiction Cinema

One way of exploring the thematic oppositions established in science fiction cinema in more detail is to look at the kinds of futures or alternatives that are imagined. Are science, technology and rationality depicted as being generally 'good' things, offering the promise of a better future? Or are they shown as potentially evil and dangerous, threatening the future of humanity? Are scientists, and the technologies they use, heroes or villains? Is their 'scientific rationality' a force for the improvement of mankind or a threat?

One strategy is to imagine a future in which science, technology and rationality hold the promise of a better world, in which our major problems can be overcome. At its most extreme this would present a *utopian** vision, a perfect, untroubled world. This perspective dates back to the scientific revolution set in motion in the sixteenth and seventeenth centuries and aided by the key writings of major figures such as Copernicus and Newton. Science is supposed to offer a means of challenging ancient superstitions, beliefs and prejudices, providing a more rational way of understanding and behaving (although it has not always been seen as incompatible with religion). In films that take the utopian approach scientists are presented as visionaries and heroes. They are clear-sighted individuals who offer a way of escaping our traditional human vices and creating better worlds.

An example of a film that presents its scientists as rational saviours of humanity is *The Day the Earth Stood Still*, in which an advanced alien power warns the Earth that it faces destruction if its domestic squabbles threaten to spread beyond the planet. The alien Klaatu (Michael Rennie), who delivers the warning, is presented as intelligent, rational and superior. The film depicts much of humanity as childish, irrational and inclined to fear and panic. Only the brilliant Professor Barnhardt (Sam Jaffe) and an array of international scientist colleagues are receptive to Klaatu's message. The film asserts the importance of rationality, of head over heart. Rationality is presented as an approach that can conquer 'irrational' behaviour and fear of the unknown. This seems to reinforce an ideological investment in the expert as potential saviour of the world, a discourse that had some currency in the 1950s, although it is often countered by a more questioning perspective.

The hero of *It Came From Outer Space* is positioned in a similar manner, protecting the alien occupants of a space ship that crash-lands for repairs from what are presented as the irrational fears of others. Rational scientists are often open to possibilities beyond those allowed by occupants of more rigid mindsets, an opposition suggested in *Quatermass and the Pit* (1967), where the scientist-hero is set up in opposition to an army that can only see terrestrial military implications in the discovery of buried alien craft. These scientists retain more distinctly 'human' characteristics, however, particularly a quirky individualism that acts as a guard against the more negative potential of the strictly rational. The scientist might be linked romantically with a woman, conventionally seen as a repository of more human and nurturing values. This is a feature of many films, including *War of the Worlds* (1953), in which the 'top man in astro and nuclear physics' (Gene Barry) is paired with a woman closely associated with 'traditional' values of pastoral community and family. Even the cool rationality of Klaatu is mitigated to some extent by his interaction with a trusting woman and her young son. Too great an emphasis on 'rationalism' can be a problem, not least for the Hollywood style of film-making, which revolves around portraits of emotional individualism. If the rationalist utopia is incompatible with certain constructions of 'the human', it also risks transgressing a basic narrative rule of Hollywood. Scepticism can be deployed here in two different ways. It might be based on scientific and rational principles, but is equally likely to be rooted in a suspicious distrust of the scientific point of view. Heroes of science fiction are often defined as such precisely because they do not accept expert testimony.

Many science fiction films include visions of utopia, but these usually prove illusory or oppressive. Dream houses turn into prisons, while rationalised and controlled worlds are liable to become lifeless totalitarian dictatorships. Few science fiction films buy very far into the rational utopian dream: technological nightmares seem to be far more common. Here we get a very different approach to issues such as science, technology and rationality. The scientists are likely to become villains rather than heroes, even if they set out with the best intentions. In many science fiction films, technology threatens not to liberate us but to take over, to dominate or even to destroy humanity. Rationality is seen as a threat to the very things that make us human, rather than a corrective to the worst parts of humanity. Everything that science, technology and rationality seemed to promise goes wrong. The bright, clear prospects of science and technology turn into a grim nightmare. Dystopia is often presented as failed utopia, as a demonstration of the dangers of attempting to engineer any kind of perfect world.

There are plenty of examples of this kind of dystopian impulse in science fiction. The whole of humanity appears to be on the verge of eclipse in the plastic, hi-tech world of *2001: A Space Odyssey*, which suggests that humanity is merely a passing stage in a larger process of evolution guided by higher powers. Rationalised and imprisoning futuristic environments are common currency in the genre with examples ranging from *Metropolis* to *THX 1138* (1970), *Logan's Run* (1976) and *Gattaca* (1997). The fully automated dream house of *Demon Seed* (1977) is a typical instance, on a small scale, of the utopian world that turns bad. The house is full of labour-saving devices, including voice-controlled doors and a domestic programme that produces soothing music and mixes a relaxing drink for the scientist Alex Harris (Fritz Weaver) when he comes home after a hard day in the laboratory. Harris has also invented a new generation of thinking computer, Proteus IV, which creates a cure for leukaemia in just a few days. This is all very life-affirming until Proteus seeks to take charge of its own destiny by holding Harris's wife (Julie Christie) prisoner, impregnating her and forcing her to give birth to its human-machine hybrid baby. On a broader scale, computer networks or machines threaten the extinction or slavery of the human species in the worlds envisioned by *The Terminator* (1984) and *The Matrix*. The latter presents a deliciously grim dystopian portrait of a near-future in which humans have been reduced to the role of batteries supplying energy to a race of machines.

Why should the dystopian version be so much more prevalent than images of utopia? One reason might be simply that better movies are made from the dark threats and destruction of technological nightmare. Any kind of realised utopia might be rather tedious, lacking the tension and conflict often basic to narrative. *Star Trek*, in its various film and television manifestations, is one product that presents a sustained vision of technologically advanced utopia, on Earth at least, where all divisions appear to have been solved. But *Star Trek* spends most of its time elsewhere, in search of the kind of adventure that is extremely hard to conjure in the halcyon groves of utopia. Large-scale spectacle, action and special effects are important aspects of contemporary science fiction, as will be discussed in Section 2, all of which lend themselves rather more immediately to the presentation of darker futures or alternatives.

This issue is taken up explicitly in *Demolition Man* (1993), set in a version of the twenty-first century in which serious crime has been eradicated. Sex, kissing, smoking, swearing, using non-educational toys and eating spicy food are among the many activities deemed illegal in the interests of a sensible rational way of life – the opposite is suggested in *Sleeper* (1973), which presents a 2173 in which steak, cream pies and hot fudge are recommended dietary items and tobacco is considered healthy. *Demolition Man* offers a parody of twentieth-century *political correctness**, but also makes a case for the values of the Hollywood action film. Police officer Lenina Huxley (Sandra Bullock) is a fan of action heroes of the past

– a poster for the film *Lethal Weapon* (1987) is among the many artefacts of forbidden twentieth-century culture on her office walls – and longs for some real action to liven up the dull routine of policing a utopia. This comes in the form of an escaped criminal from the past. Utopian niceness grows soft and flabby, the film suggests, and the twenty-first-century police are incapable of dealing with violence. The only solution is to defrost from cryogenic prison a tough-but-unconventional police officer, John Spartan (Sylvester Stallone), and let the violent action fly.

There might also be an historical explanation of the dominance of dystopian visions. As Vivian Sobchack (1993) suggests, the bulk of science fiction cinema has been produced since the dropping of the atom bomb, which demonstrated the massively destructive capacity of some scientific developments. Sobchack associates a more utopian strain in science fiction literature with an earlier period. Nightmarish science fiction films might also be a way for us to confront some of our fears about developments in science and technology. A more utopian note is struck by some representations of science 'fact'. The long-standing BBC television series *Tomorrow's World*, for example, tends towards an 'isn't it wonderful' attitude towards developments from the cutting edge of science and technology. Science fiction tends to be more suspicious, exploring the darker underside of science and articulating real fears about developments in areas such as nuclear weapons/power or genetic modification. Nightmarish visions of future or alternative worlds might also appeal to viewers as a way of making their own worlds, however troubled, seem comparatively benign.

It would be wrong, however, to suggest that most science fiction films are entirely dystopian. Unmitigated dystopia is only slightly more common than utopia – most mainstream science fiction cinema has the best of both worlds, and films often go some way towards reconciling the difference between utopian and dystopian visions. Science fiction tends to value and be excited by the possibilities of science, technology and rationality, but only up to a point. Science is portrayed as important, but as something that must be kept in check: although it is seen as intrinsic to human endeavour and curiosity, it must not become dominant or threaten the prevailing definition of humanity. It is usually only when science or technology is allowed to get out of hand that it leads towards dystopia or apocalyptic destruction. Science and technology are celebrated as long as they remain subservient to human needs. They are implicitly or explicitly celebrated every time a science fiction film presents us with great vistas of space travel or the amazing transformations performed by futuristic technologies. The measure of how far we can go along with this is the impact on our conception of humanity, as defined by prevalent *ideology**. Humanity is usually defined in science fiction in terms of an additional dimension that goes beyond the rational into realms of emotion and feeling; it may also involve unconventional behaviour and other expressions of individuality.

Independence Day (1996) is an example in which high-level technology is depicted as important but limited. Technology by itself is useless against an alien invading force; the alien force-field is immune to missile attacks or nuclear detonation. But the aliens are eventually defeated when science and technology are combined with a bunch of quirky, idiosyncratic human qualities, including the inspired uploading of a computer virus into the alien system by the off-beat genius David Levinson (Jeff Goldblum), a move explained as giving it a fatal cold. Many science fiction films present us with potentially terrifying elements of dystopia, in which the survival of humanity is under serious threat, but in most cases they negotiate an inventive way out of the ultimate gloomy fate. The qualities of humanity are usually reasserted, if only at the last gasp, and reconciled with a more controlled version of science and technology.

The two *Terminator* films offer another instructive case. The first film has a strongly dystopian tone, leaving us with the impression that humanity is barely hanging on in the future prospect of a war against the machines. *Terminator 2: Judgment Day* (1991) undoes the threat almost entirely. Starting out with images of the apocalyptic conflagration to come, the film ends up with changes brought about in the present that ensure the future will be different: the designer of the new generation of computers, which would eventually try to wipe out humanity, is convinced to destroy his work after being shown evidence of its future outcome. The

Terminator films are able to confront a technological threat to humanity, to provide the viewer with the spectacular effects that this involves, and still to assert that human values will win out in the end. An opposition between humanity and science/technology is drawn very starkly, only to become blurred, especially in the sub-plot of the sequel in which the original threatening Terminator figure (Arnold Schwarzenegger) is refigured as the perfect self-sacrificing father. *The Matrix* also presents a final triumph of the representatives of humanity, further developing the notion of a messianic figure who acts as our saviour.

In some cases the conclusions to be drawn are rather less clear-cut. *Things to Come* (1936) ends with what sounds like a plea for the importance of expanding our scientific horizons, but leaves plenty of space for a different reading. The film's vision of a gleaming underground city of the year 2036 embodies many of what have since become familiar features of the would-be utopia. This world appears to be better than its predecessor, a 1970s landscape of devastation and warring barons created by decades of war and pestilence. It is meant to represent the restoration of order and civilisation. Initially the film seems to establish character identifications that lead us to choose this prospective future over the earlier world defended by the warlord Boss (Ralph Richardson). Yet the emissary for what will become the future society dedicated to 'order', John Cabal (Raymond Massey), is presented in the somewhat sinister terms of world government and strength through gigantic air power. The science for which Cabal is spokesman is rejected by Boss as 'an enemy of everything that's natural in life'. The dice seem weighted in favour of Cabal at this stage, but less so in the latter part of the film set in a 2036 society ruled by his great-grandson, Oswald. The artist Thetocopulus (Cedric Hardwicke) starts a rebellion against 'progress', favouring 'the good old days when life was short and merry and the devil took the hindmost'. When the rebellion takes hold it resembles mob rule and is aimed at preventing the launch of a probe to be fired to the Moon by a gigantic 'spacegun'; the viewer seems to be positioned to favour successful launch rather than rebellion, if only because we want to witness the spectacle. At the same time, we are invited to accept some of

FIGURE 2 *Things to Come (1936)*

the case made by Thetocopulus. The inhabitants of the future celebrate their subterranean world and its artificial light, mocking those who were once reduced to living on the surface and had to make do with natural light from windows, but it is not clear that many viewers would share such a perspective; not to mention the warning that Cabal's rule is likely to turn increasingly oppressive and the political connotations of the name 'Oswald' in mid-1930s Britain – Oswald Mosley founded the fascist British Union of Blackshirts in 1932.

A key implication of most films that tackle questions of utopia and dystopia is that attempts to control or sanitise the messiness of 'normal' life are doomed to failure. The political implications of this are potentially mixed. There is a distinctly conservative tenor to the suggestion that any major interventions in the interest of creating a better way of life automatically translate into imprisoning tyranny. This could be read as akin to equating all versions of socialism, or any other movement seeking radical change, with the worst excesses of Stalinism or fascism. *Demolition Man*'s picture of oppression-by-tedium is played mostly for laughs, but the suggestion that a breed of violent heroes from the past is a source of much-needed vitality has an uncomfortably fascistic undertone. The film seeks to hedge its bets somewhat, however, by aligning the hero with an underground resistance movement fighting to achieve a supply of food. Mainstream films typically mix their messages when it comes to matters that touch too explicitly on the 'political', keen, as they usually are, to avoid alienating any potential audiences. Some dystopian films might be more radical in their political implications. The vision of future dystopia has the potential to be read as implicit criticism of contemporary life. Corporate capitalism, for example, is singled out for attack in the dark futures envisioned in *Alien* (1979) and *Blade Runner* (1982) (see Ryan and Kellner 1988; Penley 1990). Proteus IV in *Demon Seed* may be a menacing threat in many respects but also stands up to corporate forces, refusing to cooperate when asked to provide plans for the commercial exploitation of the sea bed.

Whatever its politics, rational control is often presented as elusive. In *Jurassic Park* (1993) a range of scientific controls is supposed to be in place to prevent the dinosaurs getting out of hand. Only females are created and all have an in-built fault: they cannot create the essential amino acid, lysine, which means they will die if not provided with a regular dose. Into this ordered world come the principles of *chaos theory** as explained by 'chaotician' Ian Malcolm (Jeff Goldblum) who predicts that 'nature will find a way' around the imposed restrictions. He is proved right, of course: once again, there would not be much of a film if everything worked according to the dictates of rational science.

Yet chaos theory is itself an attempt to apply rational understanding to shapes and events that defy predictability and the linear qualities of conventional science. Its fractal patterns, explored in the work of Benoit Mandelbrot (1982), have moved from the esoteric domain of pure mathematics to the world of popular culture, including some works of science fiction. Computer-generated fractal patterns are familiar totems of recent 'New Age' culture; their appeal is based on their ability to simultaneously embrace aspects of such seemingly different realms as art, nature and science. Some of these issues are taken up in π (1998), a low-budget independent film that draws on science fiction themes. The central character, Maximillian Cohen (Sean Gullette), is searching for predictable patterns in the movements of the stock exchange. He discovers that the universe is composed of patterns produced by random effects and not governed by a conventional structure of linear cause-and-effect. Spiralling fractals are evident in the film's recurrent images of shells, leaves, the sea, computer code and the *Mandelbrot set**. The pattern is presented as a carrier of mystical and universal significance. Given its power, from the world of nature to commerce, it is not surprising that Max's discovery is coveted by big business and a group of Hasidic Jews looking for the numeric name of God. Utopian enlightenment might be promised, but Cohen is thrown instead into a nightmarish world of conspiracy, magic and madness.

Travels in Space, Time and Scale

A key ingredient of science fiction cinema is travel through space or time. The ability to visit other or alternative worlds is a major appeal of the genre. Journeys into space or through time – or both – provide the opportunity to explore a range of issues. A shift into another galaxy or the past is a way to gain a different perspective on the concerns of our own place and time, as is a change of scale to microscopic or giant proportions. The speculative mode of science fiction has always included the potential to ask politically-informed questions about our own society. Relocating the treatment of sensitive issues to somewhere on the other side of the universe or in other dimensions is a handy way to avoid too much controversy or censorship, but much science fiction implicitly raises concerns close to home, however exotic or distant the setting. Travels in space, time and scale are also major sources of the spectacular and sensational pleasure of science fiction. Cinema has exploited the spectacular potential of space travel since its earliest days in films such as Méliès' *Le Voyage dans la Lune* (1902). Futuristic space travel offers an exhilarating sense of freedom and speed. The space ship that 'zaps' across the screen in a blazing streak of light is a joy in its own right, as is a time-travelling device such as the DeLorean car in the *Back to the Future* series (1985, 1989, 1990). Changes of scale also offer scope for the production of spectacular imagery, whether the back yard as vast jungle in *Honey, I Shrunk the Kids* (1989) or the inside of the body turned into a strange alien landscape in *Fantastic Voyage* (1966) or *InnerSpace* (1987).

Film-makers have been presented with two broad alternatives in the depiction of space travel. One option is to take a generally 'realistic' approach, in which the enterprise is shown in terms that make an effort to seem relatively plausible at the time the film is made. The other is to go for all-out fantasy, leaping directly to the imagination of capacities way beyond the bounds of current possibility. Like so many other useful distinctions, however, this one is far from entirely stable. 'Realism' and 'fantasy' are complex constructions that often overlap or interpenetrate in science fiction as elsewhere. The most 'realistic' science fiction always involves elements of fantasy, just as the wildest imaginings usually seek to establish some sense of realism or believability in their own terms.

A classic example of the realist approach is *Destination Moon* (1950), which presents itself with the sobriety of a pseudo-documentary, despite garbing its astronauts in brightly coloured suits to show off its Technicolor photography. Made years before the first rockets went into orbit, the film bases its speculative version of the lunar landscape on real pictures of the Moon's surface rather than any great exercise of the imagination. The journey proceeds slowly, even tediously, in its determination to establish a sense of solidity and believability. A similar approach is taken in this sense by the otherwise far more speculative and spectacular *2001: A Space Odyssey*, which devotes long stretches of time to establishing plausibility through the quality of its special effects. The dour approach of *Destination Moon* might be contrasted to the more lurid design of the alien landscapes envisioned in its near-contemporary *This Island Earth* (1954). The distinguishing feature may be the style in which a film is shot, or the parameters of its fictional premise. The style of *This Island Earth* remains solidly realist, the more fantastic dimension being provided by the representation of a distant world.

Flight to Mars (1951), similarly, takes us from an attempt to create a seemingly 'realistic' reconstruction of space flight to a series of more fantastic speculations about life on Mars. The way this is articulated entails a number of contradictions typical of the knots into which attempts to arrive at settled conceptions of realism can become tied. The solid 'ordinariness' of its space flight is signified by the fact that the crew wear everyday clothes rather than futuristic space suits and are untroubled by any effects such as zero gravity: they sit and stand chatting and drinking coffee just like characters from any Earth-bound drama, one of the men attempting a clichéd chat-up routine on the woman member of the crew. This is 'realistic' in one sense, making an appeal to the familiar and quotidian, while entirely 'fantastic' in another: the 'ordinary' becomes unrealistic in an extraordinary setting. *Destination Moon* makes claims towards realism by going to some trouble to take seriously the implications of zero-gravity; *Flight to Mars* takes an opposite approach. It inserts a brief line of dialogue about a gyroscopic device on the rocket that keeps everything the right way up and then ignores the issue. Which is more realistic? There is no single answer. 'Realism' is a quality that can be constructed rhetorically or asserted in different ways and that might often be secondary to budgetary considerations. The same kind of question could be asked about the Martians found in *Flight to Mars*, who turn out to be humanoid figures just like us. Is this realistic or fantastic? It gives the film a more realistic texture than might be found in a film that attempted (with limited means) to envisage aliens of fantastically different appearance, but is hardly realistic in the sense of plausibility. But, then, what is a realistic representation of something unknown? This is an issue to which we will return in the discussion of special effects in Section 2.

If no definitive distinction can be made between realism and fantasy, it is still the case that some science fiction films have a greater investment in appeals to one or the other. More overtly fantastic visions, distantly extrapolated from contemporary possibility, have tended to dominate the science fiction boom of the past two decades. The slow and painstaking style of *2001*, for example, has been utilised less frequently than the flashiness and speed of the 'space opera' tradition rejuvenated by *Star Wars*. This is often more fun; or, at least, offers a different kind of enjoyment. It is easier in works of more extreme fantasy to offer immediate thrills, action and spectacle, because there are fewer constraints on what might be included. The scope that fantasy offers for spectacle and excitement might account for a relative absence of films based around real space programmes. This issue is taken up in *The Right Stuff* (1983), in which the early American astronauts on the Mercury programme are compared with a group of jet test pilots and found wanting in traditional heroism. The astronauts are depicted as too deeply immersed in a web of technology, struggling continually to create any kind of space for individual heroics other than risking being blown up on the top of a rocket. It is significant that the only major film based on the Apollo Moon programme is *Apollo 13*, which focuses on the mission that went wrong. It is the failure of technology, in this case, that enables the astronauts to prove their worth and to validate the merits of human ingenuity in the face of impending disaster. Within the film, and in the historical reality, it is the crisis that permits the neglected space programme to regain its television audience, and much the same goes for its translation onto the cinema screen.

A third option is explored by some films: to use more or less realistic contemporary space craft upgraded just enough to permit them to indulge in an extra level of action and heroics. *Armageddon* offers a good example. The space shuttles engaged in a mission to prevent an asteroid hitting the Earth have special modifications, we are told. These enable them to perform the spectacular antics required by both the mission and the kind of Bruce Willis action vehicle that the producers have in mind, stunts that would no doubt rip any real space shuttle to shreds. And action heroes simply cannot be allowed to bounce around on alien terrain in the undignified and uncontrolled manner of those who really landed on the Moon. The crew in *Armageddon* are shown video footage of Neil Armstrong and assured that their new Directional Accelerant Spacesuit will enable them to move more freely, in a manner befitting the stars of a noisy Hollywood blockbuster.

In *The Time Machine* (1960) a Victorian inventor (Rod Taylor) does not move in space but backwards and forwards in time in his elegant, sledge-like machine. Travelling forward, he reaches a distant future in which a vicious class war is in progress. This allows the inventor to take on the guise of an action hero, prompting the gentle and downtrodden Eloi to revolt against the oppressive and exploitative Morlocks. Muscular and morally correct (Christian) science rescues future mankind from oppression. The fact that atomic science is implicated in a war that destroys London is ignored. Time travel serves here as a way to make universal claims for the particular definition of humanity dominant in the America of the mid-twentieth century. All human experience, whatever the time or culture, is reduced to a single constant. The scientist is an ingenious inventor and, like the BBC's *Dr Who* (1963–1989), the film promotes science as both a 'Boy's Own' adventure and a creative, heroic force.

Teleporting forward to the 1980s and *Back to the Future* (1985), time travel has a slightly different focus, although still implicated in the construction of an idealised version of society. When Marty McFly (Michael J Fox) travels back in time he returns to his mother's halcyon teenage years in the mid-1950s. Despite all the gizmos in the DeLorean time machine invented by Doc Brown (Christopher Lloyd), this is a very home- and family-centred film, nostalgically constructing the 1950s as more benign than the liberal or decadent 1980s, in which the local picture house has become a porn cinema. McFly's intervention in the past changes the character of his family, magically creating a future/present in which they are more sophisticated and successful. One of the pleasures of the film, understood from the perspective of psychoanalytically based theories, might involve the fantasy of witnessing, improving and having a controlling hand in our own creation, and even perhaps realising 'incestuous desires' (Penley 1990: 122). This becomes a more complex and hazardous experience in *Back to the Future Part II* (1989), in which alternate pasts and futures, not all benign, begin to multiply.

Time travel broadens the visual scope of science fiction because it allows its stars to be shown in various costume styles and interacting with important historical events. This tends to reduce history to simply a difference in visual style that is often figured in terms of film genre conventions, such as the western background to *Back to the Future Part III* (1990). History is usually fixed within the confines of one particular interpretation, despite constant warnings about the dangerous effects of tampering with the past. Time travel narratives such as *A Connecticut Yankee In King Arthur's Court* (1949), *The Navigator: A Medieval Odyssey* (1988) and *Terminator 2* often portray the fictional present as 'better', more liberal, clever and benevolent, and therefore more 'advanced' than the past or future. *La Jetée* and *Twelve Monkeys* (1995) also render their respective presents as more palatable than the alienating confines of the post-apocalyptic future. The effect is like that suggested in other cases of dystopia: however bad our own time might sometimes seem, it is positively bountiful compared with some of these alternatives. We are invited to enjoy the action, thrills and spectacle unleashed in such worlds from a position of safety. The dystopias of recent Hollywood science fiction have a seductive appeal to some viewers, combined with a sense of horror (see Barker and Brooks 1998, for interviews with a range of audience groups, especially the transcriptions on 278–80). The time travel film sometimes offers the fantasy of escape from *historical determinism** in favour of a typically Hollywood celebration of the ideology of individual freedom: 'no fate' as Sarah Connor (Linda Hamilton) writes, emphatically, in *Terminator 2*.

The dimensions of outer space and altered human scale are not always seen as distinctly separate in science fiction, the classic instance of conflation being the philosophical tone adopted in the ending of *The Incredible Shrinking Man* (1957). The tortured hero Robert Carey (Grant Williams) eventually finds peace and acceptance as he climbs out into the vast expanse of the world from the basement of the former home from which he has become estranged. 'The unbelievably small and the unbelievably vast eventually meet, like the closing of a gigantic circle', he muses, as we are presented with images of swirling galaxies. Space flight prompts a similar kind of philosophising in *Flight to Mars* when one of the scientist-astronauts proposes an equivalence between the elements that make up the vast universe and the corpuscles that

FIGURE 3 *The Incredible Shrinking Man (1957)*

comprise the interior 'universe' of the human body. Our own world can be opened up to view from radically different perspectives. A key plot element of *Men in Black* (1997) is the recovery of a lost jewel that contains an entire swirling galaxy in miniature; the film closes with a shot in which the camera pulls back hyper-kinetically to reveal our own galaxy to be nothing more than the contents of a marble in a game played by aliens.

Much of the appeal of *The Incredible Shrinking Man* and its various derivatives – including *The Incredible Shrinking Woman* (1981) and *Honey, I Shrunk the Kids* – lies in the juxtaposition of familiar figures and objects at different scales. The diminution of Carey is measured by the increasing size of domestic furniture, equipment and creatures. At one point the domestic cat is a giant, transformed into a horror film monster; a role adopted later, at another scale, by a spider. The film establishes a general sense of disorientation within familiar environments, occasionally playing tricks to keep our sense of scale uncertain. Later, we cut to a scene where, momentarily, Carey appears to have been restored to normal size, judging by the furniture, although he turns out to have moved into a doll's house. The equally tortured title figure of *The Amazing Colossal Man* (1957) finds objects capable of interesting him, at his own scale, in the shape of a giant crown and slipper that form part of the decoration on the façades of Las Vegas casinos. The *Incredible Shrinking Man* gives the narrative of changed scale an existentialist slant as Carey's series of dilemmas are used eventually to assert the indomitable nature of the 'human spirit'.

The sub-genre also has potential for forays into the world of domestic politics, a more explicit feature of *The Incredible Shrinking Woman* and the two versions of *Attack of the 50ft Woman* (1958, 1993), in which an abused wife gets her revenge on an adulterous and plotting husband after an alien encounter turns her into a giant. The original gives us little access to the interior world of the prodigious Nancy Archer (Allison Hayes), but in the remake the same character (Daryl Hannah) finds strength and peace at her new scale. These qualities are transferred to two other women characters in the remake, giving it a stronger feminist tinge, even if Archer meets the same unfortunate end in both versions. If a doll's house becomes a habitable space for the shrinking man, the 'real' world takes on toy-like proportions for the giant: cars and people can be picked up and thrown at will. In narratives of shrinkage, the ordinary becomes strange, monstrous or forbidding. Fleas are deployed as miniature weapons in *The City of Lost Children* (1995), offering scenes from a flea's perspective in which the human body becomes a vast and often grotesque spectacle. Gigantism can create similar effects from the opposite end of the scale. The terrifying 'normal' spider of *The Incredible Shrinking Man* becomes the giant ants of *Them!* (1954), the assorted bugs of *Starship Troopers* (1997), or, in order of silliness, the four-foot tall rabbits of *Night of the Lepus* (1972) and the mutant tomatoes of the parodic *Attack of the Killer Tomatoes* (1978). Science fiction has the capacity to transcend our familiar understandings of space, time and scale, potentially to raise challenging issues about the nature of the world; more often, however, these are passed over fairly rapidly in the interests of spectacular fun and entertainment.

Constructing Otherness: Artificial Intelligences, Aliens and Cyborgs

From *Metropolis* to *Manga** films, much of the dramatic and structural tension of science fiction derives from the construction of a primary difference between the 'human' and the 'other'. This difference can take diverse forms, but there are some consistent images, despite shifts in technology. In *Metropolis* the robot Maria embodies the inhuman qualities of the mechanical age. The film depicts the workers as so regimented that ideals such as love and family are subsumed under the aegis of production. The film thus provides an implicit critique of the logic of both capitalism and Stalinist communism. The robot is a ubiquitous figure in various stages of science fiction. The robot – or later the computer, android, cyborg or artificial intelligence – is rendered good if it serves human goals. Prominent examples include Robbie the robot from *Forbidden Planet* (1956), with 'his' prodigious ability to replicate any kind of material, and Data in the new generation *Star Trek*, who is deeply fascinated by human behaviour and serves the human-defined goals of Star Fleet Command. Both are tailored to obey the requirements of Isaac Asimov's manifesto for the programming of robots, the primary rule of which dictates that they must not harm humans (from the 'Handbook of Robotics', 56th edition, 2058 AD, cited in 'I, Robot', 1971).

This scheme also applies to aliens. Friendly aliens, such as those found in *Close Encounters of the Third Kind* (1977) or *E.T. The Extra-Terrestrial*, seem to serve human interests. They offer reminders of some of the specifically 'human' qualities that might be under threat on Earth. In *The Day the Earth Stood Still*, untypically, it is the need for cool rationality that is positively promoted. In *Close Encounters*, *E.T.* and *Cocoon* (1985) the opposite appears to be the case: the aliens are characterised as warm, emotional and caring and the audience is bathed in what purports to be something close to a sense of religious exaltation. The qualities offered by the aliens appear to make up for elements of family breakdown prominent in the visions some of these films provide of life on Earth, visions that come with a strong implicit politics focused on the absence of the 'natural' father. Aggressive alien colonisers in *War of the Worlds*, *Mars*

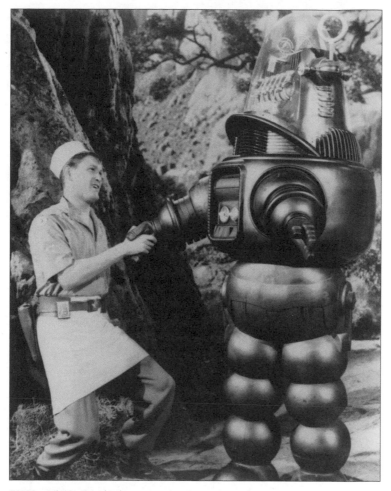

FIGURE 4 *Forbidden Planet (1956)*

Attacks!, *Independence Day*, *Invasion of the Saucer Men* (1957) and *Star Trek: First Contact* (1996) eschew human values in favour of pursuing their own usually cold and 'rational' goals. Evil aliens can be read as metaphors for a range of perceived threats to humanity, or particular groups, ranging from 1950s communism to the AIDS virus and contemporary 'illegal aliens' of human origin. The alien as lethal virus is presented in *The X Files Movie* (1998). A conflation of extra-terrestrial and terrestrial alien is common currency. *The Arrival* (1996) has its aliens set up base in Mexico, just south of the American border, and when they assume human form it is usually in a guise of Mexican appearance (see Dean 1998). Fear of 'alien intrusion' is thus given what might be seen as spurious justification as if freed of the racism implicit in its more quotidian variety, an issue played for laughs in *Men in Black* and given more complex treatment in *The Brother From Another Planet* (1984) and *Alien Nation* (1988).

The alien in *The Brother From Another Planet*, a low-budget independent film, is black, crash-landing at Manhattan's Ellis Island Immigration Centre. Ending up on the streets of Harlem, he seems more at home than either the two white-skinned aliens who pursue him or two white conference-goers who wander into the neighbourhood by accident. The alien is adopted by a supportive black culture, despite oddities such as his lack of speech, particularly when his pursuers pose as agents of the immigration service. *Alien Nation* gives us the alien 'newcomer' as an abused minority population in America; 300,000 genetically engineered workers having been stranded on earth by an intergalactic equivalent of a slave ship. As a blend of science fiction and 'cop' thriller, however, we should not be surprised that the film evades the political issues in favour of the assertion of unity at the individual level of a 'buddy' relationship between white and alien detectives.

This is a strategy typical of Hollywood production. Potentially contentious political issues form a point of reference. Their implications are not explored in detail because this is considered likely to be divisive and alienating to audiences seeking 'entertainment', which is usually understood as entailing the avoidance of explicitly 'political' material. A focus on two central characters offers both a means of avoiding the larger issue and of offering a reconciliation of the individual relationship: it is much easier to reconcile two individuals of different backgrounds than to solve social problems. The individual reconciliation offers an emotional pay-off. How this works in terms of the issues can be seen from different perspectives. The reconciliation of individual representatives of different ethnic groups (or, in this case, species) might be taken as symbolic of the possibility of a broader reconciliation of social conflict. In this view, *Alien Nation* could be seen to be engaging in a work of real cultural negotiation. The extent to which Hollywood films focus on these dynamics at the level of the individual, however, might be seen more critically, from an ideological perspective. What is offered, in this account, is a substitute for any real engagement with the issues: a device that masks real and enduring conflict through the illusion of magical reconciliation. *Alien Nation* and *The Brother From Another Planet* both resort to plots in which drugs play a central role, further underlining the potentially racist equivalence established between black and alien subcultures.

The 'good' alien of science fiction sometimes takes on the patina of a kind of God figure. Klaatu in *The Day the Earth Stood Still* adopts the name Carpenter, 'goes among the people', is killed, resurrected and ascends into the sky: clearly established as Christ-like. A similar pattern is found in *E.T.*, where the extra-terrestrial also has miraculous healing powers transferred through a glowing fingertip, a quality parodied in the magical touch of the alien in *The Brother from Another Planet*. The 'bad' alien is more like the devil, a figure literalised in *Quatermass and the Pit*; the film suggests that historical descriptions of Satan might have been based on the appearance of horned creatures from Mars. Most aliens seem to line up fairly clearly on the 'good' or 'bad' sides of the equation, but there are more equivocal cases. The guiding intelligence of *2001*, for example, takes on god-like proportions, having effectively created humankind, but is also distant and overwhelmingly strange, largely as a result of not being directly represented at all.

Since the 1960s, computers and artificial intelligences have been presented among the principal embodiments of the 'other' located within technology. Although created by humans, they sometimes develop consciousness beyond the human and, like Proteus IV in *Demon Seed*, may come to regard humanity as flawed and outmoded. The implications of AI (Artificial Intelligence) are also taken up in *Johnny Mnemonic* (1995), influenced by *cyberpunk**, in which a dead woman scientist is uploaded into a computer matrix and, as a 'ghost in the machine', haunts the chairman of an exploitative bio-chemical company. This AI works on behalf of humanity, preventing the company from withholding a cure for a fatal disease described as a product of 'technological civilisation'. Many of these films offer a simple and straightforward distinction between the human and the other, defined respectively as 'good' and 'bad'. Some obscure the distinction, to unsettling effect.

Recent science fiction has been troubled by the implications of genetic engineering and *cyborg** technology. The 'replicants' of *Blade Runner*, made in the image of humans, return to Earth to confront their maker in an attempt to reverse their in-built short life expectancy. The replicants begin to develop emotions, a key indicator of 'human' qualities. Rachael (Sean Young), a later model, has also been supplied with ersatz memories – a personal history – and is unaware of her artificial status (see Landsberg 1995). Given that Rachael is the love interest of the main character, Deckard (Harrison Ford), sympathy is created for her devastatingly ambiguous status. Further intimations, especially in the 'director's cut' version of the film, indicate that even Deckard is a replicant. In the world of genetic engineering our usual measures cannot guarantee an ability to detect 'natural' origin or identity. The thematic power of the film lies in blurring the boundary between human and replicant, creating uneasiness that is given a contemporary edge by real-world developments in cloning and other forms of genetic modification.

The figure of the cyborg has potentially liberating political dimensions, according to Donna Haraway's influential 'Manifesto for Cyborgs' (1985). Not necessarily constrained or defined by gender or biological function, the cyborg offers a means of escaping conventional identities or ideologies. This potential is rarely realised in science fiction cinema. *Blade Runner* tends to sideline any such aspects in favour of dystopian paranoia. The cyborg has often been constructed through images that offer a hyper-conformity to dominant constructions of gender, the most prominent example being the armoured muscularity of Arnold Schwarzenegger's Terminator. Haraway's argument can be applied, but only with qualification, to *Alien Resurrection* (1997). In the previous three *Alien* films the central character, Ripley (Sigourney Weaver), stands as an emblem of the human. She fights dehumanising enemies in the form of the alien and the corporation that seeks to exploit its potential for military technology. Her toughness is tempered by a 'feminine' nurturing quality that allows her to save various child surrogates (not to mention the whole of humankind). In *Alien Resurrection* Ripley is no longer quite herself. She has undergone a genetic fusion with the alien, giving her some of the attributes of the cyborg. The resulting creation is strongly informed by Ripley's basic humanity, however, which enables her to kill her alien child and also rescue and nurture the more human-looking cyborg, Call (Winona Ryder).

Ripley and Call offer a fantasy of a knowable otherness. They both embody human attributes and goals, unlike, for example, the cold and 'beyond good and evil' Borg of the *Star Trek: The Next Generation* television series (1987–1994) and *Star Trek: First Contact* (1996). Ripley and Call are not too radically other; both retain some 'feminine' characteristics alongside a kick-ass toughness. Star performers play both, a fact that limits the extent to which we are ever likely to view them as radically 'other'. Neither quite knows who they are but together, as a mother and daughter team, they save the world. They are still guided by principles of humanism and conventional gender difference, through the foregrounding of nurturing qualities, and so do not go very far towards fulfilling the premise of Haraway's radical feminist manifesto. Figures of the woman warrior can serve to question conventional definitions of 'passive' femininity. This is not to suggest that the transgression of dominant gender codes is always (or only) a radical or disruptive process; transgression, of various kinds, is sometimes offered by the mainstream film industry as part of its appeal, to lure viewers with the promise of elements that are usually forbidden. In most cases, however, an inherent conservatism – a desire not to offend potential filmgoers – ensures that mainstream productions do not transgress too far from dominant and familiar constructions of gender difference. This approach often results in a mixture that might appear incoherent, merely trying to have it all ways to appeal to a range of audiences, or as a way of seeking to reconcile major cultural differences and contradictions. Scope remains for a variety of different readings, including potentially those that contest dominant assumptions.

The threat from the terrifying aliens of the *Alien* series is compounded by the machinations of a sinister corporation. The crew are set up in *Alien*. What they believe to be a rescue mission is in fact a conspiracy hatched to bring the alien back to Earth in the hope that its prodigious military potential might be exploited; the crew are expendable. Conspiracies of one kind or another often seem to entangle alien encounters in recent science fiction. This is a central theme of *The X Files Movie* and the original television series (1993–present) but is also found to varying degrees in many other films, regardless of whether the aliens themselves are characterised as benign or threatening. In both *Close Encounters of the Third Kind* and *E.T.* the aliens make contact with ordinary Americans. This relationship is threatened by the intrusion of sinister government forces that eventually invade the domestic sanctum in *E.T.* in a manner that renders them more alien than the extra-terrestrial.

Independence Day, like *The X Files*, plays explicitly on the conspiracy lore surrounding the alleged alien crash-landing at Roswell, New Mexico in 1947. The claim that bodies were recovered, and that the truth has since been suppressed, is supported by both fictions. Like *Close Encounters* and *E.T.*, however, *Independence Day* offers a way out of the conspiratorial labyrinth. The president discovers the truth and is eventually able to restore proper democratic control. He goes to 'Area 51', sees the alien craft and the bodies, sacks a duplicitous cabinet member and leads the counter attack against alien invasion. The conspiracy is shown to be real, but also disentangled. This seems to fit the pattern of cultural products that raise difficulties only to brush them away again. Little of the kind is offered by *The X Files*. Temporary victories are achieved by Mulder and Scully, but for each dimension of the conspiracy uncovered several more appear to be generated, including at times the possibility that the underlying 'truth' about alien contact is itself no more than a cover story for other concealed government machinations. This is partly attributable to the series context of the television and cinema franchise, which requires a lengthy and on-going plot, and partly a quality inherited from the Hollywood conspiracy movies of the early 1970s.

For some alien-conspiracy theories, science fiction cinema itself is a prime ingredient in campaigns of misinformation. One widely circulated rumour is that the US government formed an alliance with the aliens that has subsequently broken down. The conspiracy theory suggests that the series of films featuring 'nice' aliens in the early 1980s was made at the time of the alliance as part of a government strategy to prepare people for the future revelation of extra-terrestrial contact. The harsher portrayal of aliens that has followed in many films is interpreted as post-alliance preparation for potential confrontation (see Dean 1998). Bruce Rux (1997) suggests, mock-seriously, that the silliness of many 1950s science fiction films was part of a deliberate misinformation strategy in which aspects of 'real' UFO-encounter information were associated with daft plots in order to discredit the whole idea of alien contact. Rux is an advocate of the theory that a long history of alien encounters can account for many of our ancient mysteries and technologies dating back at least as far as the pyramids, a line explored in *Stargate* (1994), although he would doubtless convict the film of trying to associate such important 'facts' with the stuff of idle fantasy.

Gender, Sex and Science Fiction

Genres are often seen as being gendered. With its focus sometimes on science and technology as 'toys for the boys' and its relationship to genres such as horror and the western, the appeal of science fiction might be considered chiefly to be masculine. This argument might be levelled at a recent example such as the multi-genre brew that constitutes *Starship Troopers*, a science fiction that contains distinct elements of both horror and the western. To help counter any masculine bias some science fiction films include elements of romance and melodrama, providing an address to conventional industry understandings of what attracts a female audience (for more about Hollywood's assumptions on this subject, see

Kramer 1998). *Starship Troopers* makes its own effort in this direction, including a central romantic narrative component launched in an early section that obeys the conventions of the more female-oriented high-school genre. *Star Wars* also works quite hard to appeal to a female audience through the design of the feisty character of Princess Leia (Carrie Fisher). Film viewing is a complex process and it would be a mistake to categorically label science fiction as simply a 'masculine' genre. Science fiction cinema often juxtaposes a 'masculinised' science to a 'feminised' nature or otherness, but it is important to note that films often produce contradictions in their attempts to appeal to different audiences. *Starship Troopers*, like *Aliens* (1986), presents both men and women among the tough fighting corps, even if the woman marked as the principal romantic interest for the leading man remains above the fray most of the time as the pilot of a starship.

Films can also be read 'against the grain', in ways that might not have been intended, or to bring out sub-textual themes that might not be obvious. This might be achieved through camp, *queer** or feminist-informed readings, for example, or the cult revaluation of films formerly regarded as poorly made. *Plan 9 from Outer Space* is the classic example of the latter, celebrated precisely for the endearing qualities of its trashy effects and story. The film belongs to a group of low-budget science fiction/horror hybrids in which the moral order is threatened by 'perverse monsters', which allow these films to be re-claimed as opening a 'space to figure queer desire' (Benshoff 1997: 159). Monsters in 1950s science fiction have been read as articulating a fear of homosexuality. Harry Benshoff argues that in films such as *Creature From the Black Lagoon* (1954) the monster is 'queer' because it interferes with the smooth running and consummation of heterosexual romance, a dimension ignored by critics who focus solely on the monster as a symptom of anti-communist paranoia. Benshoff argues that a fear of homosexual men who 'pass' as straight underlies the narrative of *I Married A Monster From Outer Space* (1958), in which the alien/husband prefers to meet strange men in a public park rather than stay at home with his wife. The obvious gendering of the active male hero who rescues an endangered, stiletto-wearing woman, an image prevalent in the B-movies of the 1950s, is also open to plural readings. From one perspective, this appears to be a clear and confident expression of dominant constructions of masculinity. It can also be viewed rather differently, however, exposing this brand of masculinity as an arbitrary construct in need of reinforcement through exaggerated images of male super-heroics.

It is important to consider how gender conventions inform those of genre and the intended market for science fiction, but it is equally necessary to address the operation of gender at a structural level in the text. The binary oppositions often employed in science fiction cinema are frequently gendered and it is the tension between these oppositions that provides much of the dramatic and ideological tension. Within the logic of structuralism and *psychoanalysis**, gender is first and foremost a 'relation', gaining its meaning from its relationship with other terms. The meaning of masculinity as 'active and aggressive', for example, is dependent on its difference from femininity constructed as 'passive and nurturing'. It is commonly held in psychoanalytically informed studies of gender that these differences are 'primary' oppositions that inform a wide range of discourses and narratives. In science fiction gender differences often overlap with other binary distinctions. Science and rationality are conventionally gendered as masculine and often juxtaposed with nature, the supernatural and the irrational, which are constructed as feminine. This has led some theorists to suggest that science fiction cinema can be seen partly as a response to fear of the feminine as a source of emasculation (see, for example, Creed 1993). The male hero figure, according to this reading, must prove his masculinity by defeating the alien invaders or the dehumanising force and by rescuing the besieged heroine. In this reading of science fiction all types of difference tend to be subsumed to the preservation of conventional gender roles.

This is a useful argument, but there are complications and ambiguities it does not encompass. Alien invaders are often presented as technologically-centred and tend to be rational to the point of excluding all emotion. In the likes of *War of the Worlds* and *Independence Day* the aggressors are devoid of feelings, which might be read as a critique of a certain cold and ruthless version of macho-masculinity. As Mark Jancovich suggests, 'qualities usually associated with femininity are highly valued' (1996: 28). These films tend to valorise a more caring version of masculinity that might reflect a widespread re-appraisal of masculinity, prompted partly by feminism and partly by the contradictions experienced by men between 'macho' ideals and their own desires to be more emotionally forthcoming. In *RoboCop* (1987) and *Judge Dredd* (1995), hard-nosed and goal-focused attributes eventually give way to a more gentle human(e) approach. Dredd (Sylvester Stallone) loses confidence in the system of law and his belief that he is infallible is undermined. These films offer the pleasurable fantasy of hyper-masculinity, balanced by taming or humanising the macho-cyborg-male through a programme of re-education or a symbolic rite of passage. This may be related to broader social currents, or to more immediate industrial purposes. Fans of the comic-strip Dredd considered the change a betrayal of the unrelenting 'love-to-hate-him' character, brought about purely to maintain the preferred image of a powerful star.

The female body has often provided a source of visual pleasure in science fiction. In *Forbidden Planet* the scientist's daughter Altaira (Anne Francis) is scantily clad and has one meeting with the heroic Captain (Leslie Nielson) when swimming nude in a pool. She becomes the Captain's prize for doing battle with the 'monster from the id' (an extension of the mind of her father). B-movie science fiction tends to figure a romance somewhere in between raygun battles and saving the world, although not in all cases. Women are only rarely granted senior positions on space missions and the like, although *Starship Troopers* presents one recent exception. Space may offer an escape from many terrestrial limitations, but the 'glass ceiling' usually remains in place. The women space travellers of *Flight to Mars* and *Rocketship X-M* (1950) exist primarily to provide romantic interest for male characters (and viewers). Women are often absent from the more artistically pretentious or cultish examples of 1960s and 1970s science fiction cinema such as *2001: A Space Odyssey*, *Silent Running* (1971) and *Dark Star* (1973). Debarring women from outer space appears in these cases to be seen as a way of dispensing with the more salacious (and populist) elements of the genre. Fantasy and soft-porn entries such as *Barbarella* (1968) and *Flesh Gordon* (1972) eschew 'serious' philosophical pondering, giving full rein to what a psychoanalytic perspective, or a queer reading, would see as the latent phallic and sado-masochistic motifs found in 1930s serials such as *Flash Gordon*. That serious and chaste science fiction is figured as masculine, while sexuality – often through the diverting erotic presence of a woman – is associated with the undemanding and the popular, speaks volumes about the gender constructions to which science fiction is often made to conform.

The dominant trend in science fiction is to represent women as objects of the *gaze**, as helpers to and prizes for the hero, or as 'othered' aliens. This trend began to change with the success of the Ripley character in *Alien*. *Barbarella* valiantly does battle with the black queen, but it was not until *Alien* that science fiction women really began to take situations by the horns. The hero of *Tank Girl* (1995) is never more at home than in ripped tights and at the helm of a tank, defeating the Water and Power Company with the help of mutant kangaroos. Linda Hamilton muscles-up to reprise her role as Sarah Connor in *Terminator 2*, while Dana Scully (Gillian Anderson) is the sceptical scientist juxtaposed to the intuitive and 'irrational' Fox Mulder (David Duchovny) in *The X Files*. These women have toughened-up in mind and body and are able to handle guns and life-threatening situations. Nevertheless, the role of women as nurturing mother-figures continues to persist. They fight, but often as a result of the instinct to protect children or their surrogates. This is true even of the super-rational Scully who sometimes comes to the rescue of the more child-like Mulder. Their dress, the weaponry or gadgets they use and the fact that they continue to endure various states of desperation also continue to frame women as the object of the gaze, even if in a more complex context. The very fact that we are expected to be surprised and amazed at these women's powers of endurance and quick thinking is often intrinsic to their function as spectacle.

Gender inequality has provided a central theme for a small group of more radical films. *Born in Flames* brings feminist politics to bear on science fiction, to a point at which familiar generic conventions are abandoned. Set in New York, ten years after the 'most peaceful revolution in the world', it is the story of a democracy increasingly subject to conservative forces. Activists seeking to bring together a range of oppositional groups create a women's army. The death of one of its leaders leads to the formation of a cross-class and multi-ethnic coalition that takes direct action, mainly by targeting media institutions and interrupting official news broadcasts. *Born in Flames* offers no special effects, is set in a recognisably contemporary New York and makes no use of the conventional visual languages of science fiction. It uses a documentary style for the most part, including montage sequences, speeches to camera, voice-overs and television news footage. The film also departs from mainstream conventions in its focus on collective, rather than individual, action: there is no individual hero or star. The future figured by *Born in Flames* is in fact a facsimile of American society in the early 1980s. Far from a brave new world, ten years of post-revolutionary complacency is presented as heralding a return to old gender, class and race divisions.

Reproduction is a further theme that constantly recurs in science fiction, from Dr Frankenstein's attempts to reproduce without the aid of a woman to the genetically modified babies of *Gattaca*. This theme is taken up from a feminist perspective in *The Handmaid's Tale* (1990), set in a world where most women have damaged reproductive organs and are unable to have children. The rulers see this as an Old Testament-style punishment for the decadent sins of a liberal age. In this new Christian fundamentalist society, women's roles have reverted back to an emphasis on being wives and mothers; the few fertile women are designated as 'handmaids' who produce babies for rich families. The film uses a science fiction format to warn against the backlash against feminism, although the upbeat ending in which Kate (Natasha Richardson) manages to escape to the hills without surrendering her baby to the surrogate family has been seen, by feminist critics, as weakening the film's message. *The Handmaid's Tale* has also been criticised for failing to take a sufficient interest in science fiction as a form, merely using it as a vehicle for political comment (see Hardy 1995). Science fiction stories written by women have found it harder to make it to the screen, which might suggest that, for all its tough women, contemporary science fiction cinema remains largely a genre that plays out male fantasies of sex and power. This is, of course, debatable. It does not follow that the gender of the author of source material necessarily determines in all ways the gender implications of what appears on screen.

Madmen, Sceptics and Nerds: Images of the Scientist

Benign boffins do their best to help humanity; crazed lunatics play Promethean games with humanity and the fabric of the universe; and those poor nerdy cerebral types sometimes need to summon more muscular heroics if they are to save the day. Science fiction cinema offers scientists in a range of guises, from good and bad to somewhere in between, from rigorous rationalist to completely nutty professor. How exactly the scientist is figured is often a good indication of the more general approach of a film, and they tend to turn up in cyclical patterns.

The benign and altruistic version of the scientist proliferated from the 1950s when some science fiction cinema, taking its lead from *Destination Moon*, branched away from the horror film. Scientists such as Professor Barnhardt in *The Day the Earth Stood Still*, Quatermass in *The Quatermass Xperiment* (1955) and Mr Spock in the original *Star Trek* utter the voice of rationality. Such figures represent progress and a spirit of curiosity, although, as we have seen, the rationality of the scientist is often balanced by careful emphasis on more specifically 'human' qualities such as individualism, emotion or romantic pairing. Scientists such as the intrepid time-traveller in *The Time Machine* are prepared to risk ridicule from their contemporaries in order to push forward the limits of knowledge. In *Brainstorm* (1983), Michael Brace (Christopher Walken) is a *passionate* man of science, not suffering from any excess of cool detachment. Such characters are thus clearly distinguished from the brilliant but unfeeling intelligences of overly rational scientists or aliens. Spock (Leonard Nimoy) is in many ways a perfect illustration, a Vulcan/human hybrid who embodies the contradictory imperatives of strict logic and humanity in a manner that makes explicit a wider tendency in the depiction of the benign rationalist.

Another widely used strategy is to combine the rational with the attributes of the absent-minded professor, a mix found in the protagonist of the first Dr Who film, *Dr Who and the Daleks* (1965) and the wacky inventor Doc Brown in *Back to the Future*. A dose of homely eccentricity makes the expert seem more vulnerably human and is a good way, perhaps, of inoculating the use of science and technology against the darker implications that often come when it is associated with threatening state, corporate or military institutions. Many scientists are far from 'macho' in the physical sense: brains tend to exceed cyborgian-brawn. They are often figured as 'good fathers' whose attraction to the arcane world of science may be either an extension of, or in conflict with, their roles as caring parents or surrogates, as is the case with Brace in *Brainstorm* and the good doctor in *Dr Who and the Daleks*.

The benign scientist can be led astray, however. The hazards of tampering with time or nature are mostly averted in favour of comic adventure, as in *Back to the Future* or *Honey, I Shrunk the Kids*. But good intentions and idealistic visions can bring about disastrous consequences. Characters whose work goes astray in this manner are apparent in the paranoid B-movies of the 1950s, standing in perhaps for those deemed to be 'misguidedly' sympathetic to communism. Such a scientist is the idealistic Tom Anderson (Lee van Cleef) in *It Conquered the World* (1956), who facilitates the arrival of a monster on Earth with the initial intention of making it a better place. Science itself is still seen as a necessary and progressive force here, even if one that can have unforeseen effects. Well-intentioned scientists who bring about disaster often start out in lofty pursuit of cures for human diseases, as we saw in *Demon Seed*. The unforeseen effects have consequences for both the characters and the generic location of the films in which they appear.

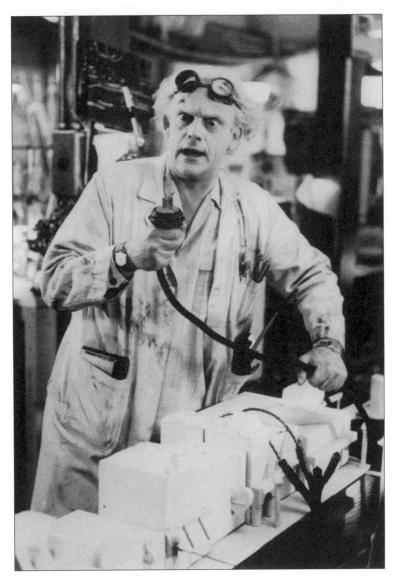

FIGURE 5 *Back to the Future (1985)*

When things start to go wrong, *Demon Seed* hovers on the border between science fiction and horror. A similar fate befalls *Mimic* (1997): a 'miracle' cure prevents the spread of a lethal childhood disease but unleashes a monstrous predator. In *Deep Blue Sea* (1999) the scientist's genetic experiments on sharks are intended to harvest a cure for Alzheimer's disease but have consequences that lead the film from aspects of science fiction to the noisy action thriller.

The scientist can also be presented in much darker terms. The protagonists of earlier films often derived from the classical horror tradition. The scientists of Fritz Lang's *Metropolis* and *The Testament of Dr Mabuse* (1933) are essentially black magicians who conjure the forces of nature and industry to fulfil their evil intentions. These, and later maniacal scientists, carry the gothic legacy of Dr Frankenstein and Dr Jekyll. Krank (Daniel Emilfork) in *The City of Lost Children* is a Frankenstein figure who has no imaginary world of his own. He abducts children and uses baroque technologies to capture and experience their dreams, making him an exaggerated fairy tale version of the coldly rationalist scientist. The unnatural exploits of the 'mad scientist' – whose goal is often to produce a robot, monster or synthetic human – unites science fiction and horror in an unholy marriage. In *Voodoo Woman* (1957) the male scientist uses white science and black voodoo to create his ideal woman. In *Mad Love* (1935) science becomes a fiendish tool with which the scientist exacts revenge for his unrequited love. The untamed desire for knowledge can lead to an active disregard for human life, as with the scientist in the 1951 version of *The Thing*, who suggests that the occupants of an Arctic survey station should be prepared to die rather than kill a threatening alien visitor from which humanity might have much to learn. The mad scientist has persisted as a staple of more recent science fiction films, including Dr Weir (Sam Neill) in *Event Horizon*. Mad scientists have a habit of spawning monsters, sometimes intentionally, as with the miniature test-tube people and the bride created in *Bride of Frankenstein* (1935), sometimes unintentionally, the classic case being the 'monster from the id' unleashed by Morbius in *Forbidden Planet*. The genetic scientist and entrepreneur responsible for the manufacture of the replicants in *Blade Runner* takes up the legacy of Morbius and Frankenstein; like them he comes to suffer at the hands of his unnatural creation.

Male scientists in films such as *Blade Runner* and *Forbidden Planet* may be interpreted as representatives of patriarchy, the status quo or the particular vested interests of capitalism. Traditionally the voice of rationalism and science is male, but in a few contemporary science fiction films this voice is assigned to women, who are often presented as combining it with a more caring and 'human' approach to science. As elsewhere, a key characteristic of these representations is an effort to have it both ways, to give at least the appearance of resolving the contradictions. Ellie Arroway (Jodie Foster) in *Contact* (1997) is a scientist in search of extra-terrestrial life. Such an enterprise is considered crazy by the scientific establishment, a waste of potential brilliance. Arroway proceeds with a rigorous scientific attitude, however, as if to make up for the marginal nature of the object of her studies. She flatly refuses to allow any religious dimension to enter the equation when extra-terrestrial life is discovered, in the process jeopardising her own opportunity to go on a mission across the galaxy. When Arroway eventually completes the journey, she is left with no evidence that it happened, and is thus forced to fall back on something closer to the kind of 'faith' she previously disparaged. Contradictions between religious belief and scientific understanding are wished away, an action cemented in true Hollywood fashion by the romantic coupling of Arroway and the handsome figure of a kind of secular priest. Drawing on contemporary cultural investments in mysticism, as opposed to empirically-based knowledge, Arroway undergoes a rite of passage into seeing things 'both ways'; a dual focus sometimes offered to Dana Scully in *The X Files*.

The misguided Frankensteinian genius who succumbs to the seductions of knowledge and power remains a conspicuous figure in contemporary science fiction. One example is Dr Angelo (Pierce Brosnan) in *The Lawnmower Man*, a researcher into the potential of virtual reality. His experiments into the expansion of mental capacities offer a potentially transcendent breakthrough in the improvement of human lives. Two factors conspire to threaten disaster, however. One is the sinister military corporation, which wants to use his discoveries for the pursuit of power, death and destruction rather than ennoblement. The corporation, Virtual Space Industries, is a typical science fiction manifestation of the evil force that subverts the scientific version of the utopian dream – one way of absolving science and the scientist from the blame when things go wrong. A second factor is Angelo's own arrogance and desire, his problems with the corporation tempting him into unofficial and somewhat unethical experiments on a dim-witted human subject.

While the Frankenstein figure suffers nobly for tampering with the laws of nature, the computer geek of many recent science fiction films is a nocturnal creature often lacking the moral integrity of Mary Shelley's tragic hero. The archetypal nerd is found in *Jurassic Park* in the form of one Dennis Nedry (an anagram of 'nerdy'), a programmer in charge of the computer that controls the park. His workstation is littered with coke cans, crisp packets and candy-bar wrappers. Overweight, lazy, greedy for junk food and money, he fulfils the stereotypical attributes of the computer nerd. Lacking both nutritional and moral fibre, he becomes the main catalyst for the disastrous release of the dinosaurs. Like many other nerds in popular culture, Nedry is not wantonly malicious but creates mayhem because he is self-centred and out of touch with the real-world effects of his actions.

Why should nerds be presented in such negative terms? What threats do they represent? One explanation is that they are striking symbols of the potential for a fascination with technology, and technological facility, to over-ride more 'human' interaction. Nerds have access to the mysterious closed world of computer technology, which can have mixed implications. They are able to navigate the technological complexities of the digital world, where a more muscular and physical hero is unable to go. The nerd has, therefore, a certain sub-cultural and subversive power and expertise that could potentially threaten the status quo. Contemporary science fiction, in response, seems equivocal in its representation of those with high levels of computer expertise. In return for one version of techno-power the nerd is given all the attributes of social and moral ineptitude.

There is a significant group of films in which the computer 'hacker' becomes a glamorous sub-cultural icon, however, as in *Wargames* (1983), *Hackers* (1995) and *Johnny Mnemonic*. The ultimate hacker, is Neo (Keanu Reeves) in *The Matrix*, who learns to defy the usual rules within an otherwise imprisoning computer-generated world. To a small band of fellow hackers, he proves to be the sought-after figure known as 'The One'. For us, the exploits of Neo and his female counterpart Trinity (Carrie-Anne Moss) are the source of an abundance of fantastic action thrills. The very term 'hacker' carries positive associations, suggesting a more sophisticated, rebellious and less smugly conformist figure than the indulgent nerd. The issue, then, is not just access to these domains, but the kind of attitude that accompanies it. A negotiation of these terms is made in *Jurassic Park*. Nedry is the nerd of nerds, but the young girl, Lex, is able to stop screaming and come to the rescue in one scene because of her computer skills. Earlier, during an argument with her brother, she resists the label 'nerd', insisting instead that she be called a 'hacker'.

The distinction may not be an absolute one and is another indicator of the different aspects of such questions that are opened up for exploration in science fiction. The presentation of the physically weak boffin or nerd appears to have shifted to some extent in recent years. Science fiction, along with its genre hybrids, has a long history of more 'geeky' figures, usually not the principal heroes, ranging from Brains in *Thunderbirds* (1963–1967) to Q in the James Bond films and the trio who offer expert backup to Mulder and Scully in *The X Files Movie* and series. The traditional geek is not a figure of muscular capacity and often does not require such prowess. Neo in *The Matrix* offers some reconciliation of the opposition between physical and mental powers. He is slightly built, which is of little relevance to skills deployed within the computer simulation. Physicality – or the 'meat', as the body is often termed in cyber-speak – is left strapped to a chair in the 'real world' dystopia. The fight scenes are highly stylised, choreographed by an expert from the martial arts cinema of Hong Kong and dependent on cinematic trickery such as expressive editing and slow motion effects. The action heroics of Neo are not 'real' within the fictional world; neither are those of the actor

Keanu Reeves in front of the camera. Yet the dominant impression offered to the viewer is the spectacle of highly physical antics within the matrix that sometimes leave their mark on the recumbent body in what the film presents as 'reality'. Neo has the best of both worlds, hacker brain and seemingly corporeal action-heroics, with an emphasis on the body as performance. This can be understood as an implicit attempt to resolve the differences between the two, or to construct a particular kind of Hollywood star image: Reeves as both the vulnerable, sensitive male and hyper-dynamic bodily presence. The martial arts context sanctions the pleasure offered by Neo to both the heterosexual male and female gaze.

The expert, the inventor, the scientist and the hacker/nerd are ubiquitous figures in the cinema of science fiction. They are often responsible for all kinds of mayhem, but they can also be the brains and the brawn behind the action, and might even be presented as humanity's saviour.

Horror and Science Fiction

Many science fiction films draw on aspects of the horror genre and vice versa (see, for a fuller description, Tudor 1989; Creed 1993). There is often a conflation of the genres in Hollywood films of the 1930s such as *Frankenstein* (1931), *Dr Jekyll and Mr Hyde* (1932) and *The Invisible Man* (1933). This has caused some confusion for critics looking to make a hard distinction between the two genres, an area in which much ink has been spilt. Mark Jancovich (1996) addresses the overlap between genres through the concept of hybridisation, suggesting that 1950s invasion narratives draw from the genre conventions of both horror and science fiction. A large number of science fiction films share with horror the presence of a monster. The distinction is far from clear-cut but often lies in the fact that the monster in the horror film has supernatural origins, while those found in science fiction tend to come from outer space or to be produced by activities such as nuclear testing or the work of the diabolical scientist. Films such as *Invasion of the Body Snatchers*,

Videodrome, *Event Horizon* and *The Fly* (1986) borrow more than just the monster motif from horror, mixing a range of thematic conventions from both genres. What these and other films have in common is that the invading agent (technology, aliens or super-human cyborgs) threatens humanity and the human body at a personal level. The films hinge around a number of anxieties, especially depersonalisation and rapid changes in bodily form, both of which express fears about loss of self-control and individuality: themes that are prevalent in both science fiction and horror.

The narrative of *Invasion of the Body Snatchers* shifts the staple horror movie zombie from the domain of the supernatural into the world of extra-terrestrial invasion. The inhabitants of an American town are gradually replaced by simulacra grown from pods. They look and sound as they did before, but lack the emotional features apparent to friends and relatives. There are no conclusive raygun or aerial battles with alien saucers; instead, the horror of alien invasion is located within domestic space and renders the familiar uncanny. The original version can be read in terms of the air of paranoia created by McCarthyite America in the 1950s, while the remake evokes something of the 1970s post-Watergate era. Both versions leave the end open and the threat unchecked. The process of possession suggested in these films threatens to destabilise familiar distinctions between self and other, human and alien. Another example of this tendency is *Quatermass and the Pit*, in which people kill one another *en masse* after being taken over by the memories of ancient locust-creatures from Mars.

The very intimate and individually targeted intrusive violations of David Cronenberg's *Videodrome*, *The Fly* and *Scanners* (1980) bring the full gamut of body-horror *tropes** to science fiction. Cronenberg envisions the impact of technology on the body in terms of evolution into a hybrid form. The body itself is the site of horror and the viewer is invited to address the fact that human bodies are never entirely under our own control. The body, according to certain precepts of Western 'rationality', is meant to be subjugated to the mind. Psychoanalytic theory is not alone in arguing that this is an illusory, if necessary, fiction. The human body is in a constant

51

state of change, at times undergoing rapid transformation, although this is something we tend to ignore in our daily lives. Body horror, from this perspective, can be seen to address latent or subconscious fears of a lack of bodily control, appending such fears to classic science fiction narratives of invasion. The central characters in *Videodrome* and *The Fly* undergo radical and terrifying anatomical changes beyond their control, threatening their identity from within. Technology is instrumental to these bodily transformations, which might be seen as a threatening evolutionary leap into the 'post-human' that makes human values such as autonomy and individuality redundant.

Science fiction approaches technology in a variety of ways. Technology itself is often treated as largely neutral, suggesting that it is primarily the use to which it is put that renders it good or bad: the question is left in the domain of human action. Some films suggest that technology can become a desiring entity in its own right, moving beyond human control. Many science fiction/horror hybrids fall into this category, including *Event Horizon*, *Demon Seed*, and *Videodrome*. The technologically embodied monsters of these films often exhibit perverse sexual desires and are figured in the mode of the gothic monster. The world of technology is subject to accelerated change that makes it unpredictable and difficult to comprehend, contributing to suspicions about the effects it might have on our lives; particularly technologies such as genetic engineering that impact directly on the body. Science fiction/horror hybrids draw strongly on these anxieties, potentially enabling them to create the kind of visceral fear that defines the horror film.

Event Horizon offers a good illustration of this generic mixture. It deploys spectacular images of space and leans on pseudo-scientific theory; these are blended with the shock tactics of the horror film through bloody images of torture, a tension-heightening music track and sudden noises calculated to startle the viewer. The film tacitly evokes the work of cult 'cosmic horror' writer H.P. Lovecraft (1890–1937), whose stories were published in science fiction/fantasy magazines such as *Amazing Stories* (1926–1995, 1997 to present) and *Weird Tales*. In the depths of space – where we all know no one can hear you scream and which provides, potentially, an allegory for the deepest levels of the mind – there lurk, in Lovecraftean terminology, the 'Old Ones', who represent the forces of chaos and destruction. The new technology carried on the Event Horizon spacecraft creates a gateway in the fabric of space and time. On returning through this gateway the Event Horizon becomes suffused with demonic forces, which begin to affect the investigating crew, damning them to murder and violent self-mutilation (Krzywinska 2000). The crime that brings forth these unnameable forces is the transgression of the space-time continuum. The order of the universe is disrupted; chaos and destruction ensue. The film brings to gory fruition the warning provided by Mary Shelley's novel *Frankenstein* (1818) that to break the rules of nature is to bring about what the Greeks called *nemesis*, which involves, at least, the death of the transgressor. *Event Horizon* is not just an intimate Oedipal battle between creator and creature; the scientist has opened the doors to an apocalyptic force that does not simply wipe out individuals in a split second of armageddon, but drives them fury-mad before pulling their bodies apart limb from limb.

Science fiction/horror hybrids such as *Event Horizon* bring the millennial fear of Judgement Day into the hi-tech present, a quality also found to some extent in the science fiction/disaster blends that characterise *Deep Impact* and *Armageddon*. *Demon Seed* and later genre hybrids such as *The X Files* and *Buffy The Vampire Slayer* (1997–present) also resurrect medieval ideas, such as demonology and the supernatural, often through the rendering of technology as personified, conscious and demonic. Re-wrapped in hi-tech chrome and silicone, age-old chthonic and gothic terrors return to haunt computer games, the internet and outer space. Imaginations of the present or the future are sometimes shaped in the mould of supernatural terrors from the past. This provides an opportunity to anthropomorphise technology, a quality that enables it to fit neatly into the character-centred narrative logic dominant in the commercial cinema. It also gives reign to manifestations of special effects, another key ingredient of recent science fiction. This tendency also draws explicitly on psychoanalytic ideas of repression and the irrational quality of the unconscious, ideas that have been taken up by horror and science fiction themselves as well as by numerous academic commentators.

Science Fiction and the Postmodern

Lines are blurred. Important distinctions become unclear. Science fiction sometimes presents a world that threatens to undermine some of the major categories into which we organise our lives. The cyborg is neither human nor machine, but something in between. The difference is not always easy to tell. Gender boundaries can also be destabilised in these cases, especially when humanity is shown to be subject to construction and reconstruction. 'Reality' is sometimes thrown into question, especially in science fiction cinema that deals with the subject of virtual reality. Virtual realities are computer-generated worlds that, in science fiction at least, can be inhabited as if they were real. They are often presented as seductive fantasies that can come to seem more real than reality itself, as in *The Matrix*. The world presented by this kind of science fiction has much in common with what has been described as a 'postmodern' condition.

The concept of the postmodern is a tricky and often confusing one, largely because so many different versions of the postmodern have been described in disciplines ranging from art and philosophy to science and economics. We will not attempt here to give anything like a definitive version of the postmodern, merely to indicate some of the ways it has been used in reference to science fiction films. One place to start is with the example of a film that provided a key point of reference in the mushrooming of studies of the postmodern that occurred in the 1980s: *Blade Runner*, a film that has influenced many subsequent science fictions.

How, then, is *Blade Runner* seen as an exemplar of the postmodern? We can begin by considering a number of boundaries the film appears to blur or confuse, a commonly cited characteristic of the postmodern. The replicants, described paradoxically as 'more human than human', threaten to undermine our fundamental distinction between human and machine.

Blade Runner also mixes up any clear sense of time. The film is clearly meant to be set in the future. But it also uses conventions normally associated with the past; the look and feel of 1940s film noir is an important ingredient, for example. The future is not imagined as bright, gleaming and progressive, but as something that has ingrown or turned back on itself. This, again, is the kind of thing said to characterise the postmodern: a loss of clear historical perspective, a juxtaposition of detail from different periods (see Jameson 1991). The two *Terminator* films might also be cited as examples of temporal confusion, based as they are on paradoxes in which the relationship between present, past and future becomes unstable; or the *Star Wars* films, with their sense of a futuristic world that is actually set in the past. More generally, the postmodern is often understood in terms of a loss of faith in progress, science or rationality (see Lyotard 1984), a recurring feature of dystopian science fiction.

These arguments might also be applied to the many contemporary science fiction films that draw on earlier products of the genre in their style or content. A common term in the vocabulary of postmodernism is *pastiche**, a concept that seems relevant to recent films that recycle science fiction films and television shows from the 1950s or 1960s. An example might be *Lost in Space*, which merely dresses up the old formula in a new technological garb. *Mars Attacks!* might appear to be another candidate for this status, although it has a more critical edge in its relationship to the 1950s films to which it plays homage, a quality Jameson takes as a crucial distinction. Postmodern pastiche is characterised as flat and uncritical, lacking the political bite of parody or satire (see Jameson 1985). The culture of the postmodern is seen as one in which there are few, if any, new ideas, merely an endless recycling of the past – something of which contemporary Hollywood science fiction is often accused.

Space, as well as time, is often said to have been transformed in the postmodern. Classic science fiction, for Vivian Sobchack (1993), presents space as something to be penetrated or explored. Science fiction that exhibits features of the postmodern is said to present space as 'flattened', or reduced to a jamboree of visual styles. Much of the fascination of *Blade*

Runner has been attributed to its surface texture, the immense volume of detail that fills the frame. In contrast, 1980s films such as *Tron* (1982) and *The Last Starfighter* (1984) reduce much of their space to the dimensions of the computer screen. The geography of *Blade Runner* also appears to blur distinctions. It is set in Los Angeles, but a version of the city that is peopled with a multi-national and multi-ethnic 'mish-mash' of peoples and languages, precisely the kind of qualities attributed to a postmodern diasporic geography of the real world (Bruno 1990; Soja 1989). Architecture is a field in which some conceptions of the postmodern were first described, postmodern architecture being defined as a style that incorporates references to all sorts of different periods or designs. *Blade Runner*, again, has been seen as an example of this approach, mixing the hi-tech, the decrepit and elements taken from an array of ancient and modern cultures (see Bruno 1990).

The disorientation created by the postmodern experience is described by Jameson in terms of a kind of *schizophrenia** that can also be read into some works of science fiction. The schizophrenic lives in a 'perpetual present', rather than with any clear relationship to the past or future. This is characterised as a world of heightened intensity, but one in which a clear sense of reality is lost. For some, this might be a description of much contemporary science fiction: a world of intense and luminous visions – of new worlds, new technologies or the transformation sequences of *Terminator* 2 – that shine brightly from the screen with an intensity that can unsettle our sense of the boundaries of reality.

The postmodern remains a contentious subject. Many of the claims made in its name are open to question. It is far from clear that the epochal changes described in some accounts have much basis in reality. They sometimes appear in a pseudo-prophetic and cautionary form that has been termed ficto-criticism. This is another point of boundary confusion, perhaps one at which social theory can slip into a mode closer to that of science fiction: the strongest example is provided by some of the wilder speculations of the French theorist Jean Baudrillard. This might be why science fiction films have proved such fertile territory for analysts of the postmodern. The theory appears to have some grasp on the world of contemporary science fiction, whatever its status in the world beyond the screen.

Even within science fiction, it is easy to overstate the extent to which boundaries such as those between reality and fantasy are really blurred. Films about virtual reality may play with our sense of which is which, but such doubts are usually resolved quite clearly in favour of one level that is established as the unquestionably real. Mainstream films in particular are constrained by a commercial demand for a certain level of narrative clarity, particularly in such fundamentals, that limits how far they can go in this respect. *The Matrix*, for example, leaves us in no doubt where reality lies, for all the seductive qualities of its presentation of the computer-generated fake. Greater leeway for sustained confusion is permitted in quirkier and more economically marginal and cultish films such as David Cronenberg's *Videodrome* or *eXistenZ*. The same could be said of the suggestion that science fiction cinema exhibits a postmodern erosion of distinctions between the human and the non-human. This is a feature of recent science fiction, but the bulk of mainstream films devote much of their energy to re-establishing a clear-cut sense of the human. Creations such as the cyborg carry the potential to undermine conventional gender roles but are used more often to assert fairly rigid distinctions. Gaps and openings are created in many of the films considered in the first part of this book, but not to the sweeping extent sometimes implied in the name of the postmodern.

2   INDUSTRIAL LIGHT AND MAGIC

Science Fiction, Spectacle and the 'New Hollywood'

Why has science fiction become so dominant on the big screen? Part of
the answer to this question has already been suggested: science fiction
cinema has relevance to a number of contemporary issues surrounding
the meanings and implications of science and technology. It offers the
pleasures of excitement, fantasy and escape, while also grappling with
some of the oldest questions about what it is to be human. Examining the
themes of science fiction cinema is important, but this does not provide a
complete answer. To understand why science fiction has become such a
prominent cultural phenomenon we also need to look at the industrial
context within which these films are produced, particularly in the case of
Hollywood. Mainstream film production is an industry; a large-scale,
expensive business, and huge sums of money are invested in today's
science fiction extravaganzas. The makers of films aimed at big audiences
need to take account of thematic issues likely to engage the targeted
range of viewers, but there is no guarantee that pressing social concerns
are automatically translated onto the big screen. The appeal of science
fiction lies in its ability to relate to such issues, while also fitting closely
into the particular kind of production favoured by the industrial terrain of
contemporary Hollywood. The contours of this landscape favour the kind
of spectacular film-making to which science fiction is ideally suited.

Bright lights buzz through the sky at hyper-speeds; a vast 'mothership' descends from the heavens, filling the screen with a multicoloured light show. Human witnesses gaze upwards, mouths open in wonder; scientists and ordinary people are united in their shared amazement. These familiar images from *Close Encounters of the Third Kind*, one of the key films in the late 1970s boom in science fiction, represent in microcosm a vision of the spectacular appeal of blockbuster science fiction cinema. They offer dazzling displays of light, colour and motion that can be enjoyed for their own sake, regardless of their relevance to the details of plot or underlying narrative themes. This is science fiction as something close to pure spectacle: a glorious larger-than-life extravaganza to watch and enjoy for sensory pleasure. At its most extreme this can be an almost abstract delight – evident in *2001: A Space Odyssey* – in the experience of gazing at previously unimaginable vistas, new dimensions or breathtaking displays of sheer energy. Spectacle of this kind has always been an important part of the appeal of cinema, from the very first films at the end of the nineteenth century, but spectacle has become especially important to the Hollywood style of mainstream commercial cinema in recent decades.

Hollywood faced a number of challenges in the 1950s. Much of its former audience was lost in the face of social changes and the growth in forms of entertainment based around the home rather than going out to the cinema, a series of developments in which the spread of television was only one factor. At the same time, the old *vertically integrated** Hollywood studio system came apart at the seams, partly because there was no longer such a big market to serve and partly as a result of direct government action against anti-competitive practices (see, for example, Balio 1990; Hillier 1993). Hollywood responded to a new climate of uncertainty in various ways. One answer was to try to appeal to a variety of smaller 'niche' audiences. This business strategy encouraged a range of different approaches to the production of science fiction. These ranged from the low-budget, high-profit drive-in movies of Roger Corman (*It Conquered the World*, *Attack of the Crab Monsters* (1957)) to the effects-plus-philosophy recipe of auteurist directors such as Stanley Kubrick

(*2001: A Space Odyssey*), John Boorman (*Zardoz* (1973)) and David Cronenberg. The appeal to niche markets helped shape the different approaches taken to science fiction cinema, a legacy apparent today in the contrast between the lurid *Mars Attacks!* and the more cerebral *Gattaca*.

Another strategy, with important implications for science fiction, was to focus increasingly on the dimension of large-scale audio-visual spectacle: one thing that might draw people out of their homes in the suburbs, away from their television sets, barbecues and outdoor leisure pursuits. The 1950s saw an increase in the production of spectacular cinema, mainly in the form of historical epics, musicals and upmarket westerns. This was the decade in which science fiction came of age in Hollywood, offering extravagances of its own, although at this stage they remained mostly relatively low-budget affairs (there were earlier examples of lavish science fiction productions, especially *The Mysterious Island* (1929)). Some of the 1950s films were more expensive and prestigious projects than average, examples including *War of the Worlds* and *The Day the Earth Stood Still*. But it was in the 1970s that science fiction shifted systematically into the first rank of expensive spectacular production. To understand how and why this happened we need to look at the development of a phenomenon that has become a familiar part of Hollywood in general and of science fiction cinema in particular: the 'blockbuster' attraction.

Blockbusters

Star Wars is generally recognised to have been the first real science fiction blockbuster, even if its potential was little realised during production. But what exactly do we mean by the term? Mainstream features that usually cost enormous sums to make and earn vast amounts of money; films that aspire to have an impact beyond the normal confines of cinema and regular cinemagoers. The ultimate success for a blockbuster is to achieve the legendary status of an 'event movie', one that imposes itself on our lives with saturation promotion and becomes for a time almost impossible to ignore. Blockbusters of this kind are the stuff of production executives' dreams.

Not all big-budget spectaculars succeed in this, of course. Some do well enough, without translating into broader events in the popular culture of their day. Others are simply black holes that suck in millions of dollars and produce little return. *Waterworld* (1995), for example, cost approximately $175 million and grossed less that half of that figure in the US market.

There has always been an equivalent of the blockbuster, from the Italian historical epics of the 1910s to *The Birth of a Nation* (1915) and *Gone with the Wind* (1939). What has changed in the *'New Hollywood'** of today is the degree of importance given to these films in the overall industrial strategy. In the heyday of the studio system, approximately from the late 1920s to the early 1950s, Hollywood made its money by churning out a large number of films of comparatively modest budget which provided a fairly steady and regulated income, even though the more prestigious 'A' feature releases in first-run metropolitan theatres accounted for a disproportionately large share.

Currently things are more abrupt and haphazard. The big studios depend on what they hope will be the huge success of a relatively small number of blockbusters, a large proportion of which can be classified as science fiction. Lower-budget 'smaller' films are still made, including plenty of science fiction. These kinds of films offer a degree of stability to the industry as a whole, their budgets and potential income not large enough for any individual titles to threaten the balance of the system within which they are produced. But the fates of the big name studios in their roles as financiers and distributors tend to ride on the success or failure of their blockbuster attractions. A single big hit can make the difference in any one year, a role that has been performed by works of science fiction far more than any other genre.

An important feature of the contemporary blockbuster is that it is usually designed to make profits beyond the cinema box office, another factor that has helped to put science fiction high in the pecking order. Today's blockbusters often make most of their money after finishing their initial run in the cinema. Heavier profits are usually made in later television and video sales. Other spin-offs include the development of merchandising products such as model figures, toys and branded clothing. Computer games and theme park rides are additional ways of extending the profits that can be squeezed from successful films. These are forms to which science fiction films are often particularly well suited. The apparently 'secondary' sources of profit available to blockbuster science fiction films are designed to stabilise an otherwise unpredictable industry, to go as far as possible to 'guarantee' a decent return on enormous budgets. The original *Star Wars* earned vastly more profits through merchandising than its record-breaking box-office returns; even *Waterworld* is reckoned to have earned its keep eventually after sales overseas and on television and video.

The huge budgets associated with blockbuster production tend to go hand-in-hand with further strategies designed to minimise risk. Many of these films are *pre-sold**, another factor that has worked in the favour of science fiction. A wealth of older science fiction materials have been scooped up from television, comic books, novels and short stories and turned into blockbuster films on the assumption that they are properties that will already possess the familiarity and recognisability deemed so important in the blockbuster arena. Examples are numerous, including the *Star Trek* films, *Judge Dredd*, *Lost in Space* and *X-Men* (2000). Science fiction has a particularly rich heritage of this kind upon which to draw, maybe because of its perceived status as a predominantly 'juvenile' form. Plenty of texts originally targeted at children or teenagers are available to be recycled in big-budget format, aimed in part at those for whom the originals have become the stuff of fond nostalgia. Science fiction films also play on a sense of contemporaneity that fits into the blockbuster strategy. They showcase and/or warn about the latest technologies – military, consumer or communications. In so doing they risk becoming rapidly out of date, but they compensate for this by demanding to be seen 'now', immediately, during what are in most cases relatively short runs in the cinema and when they are stocked in large numbers in video stores or receive premiere screenings on television.

Science fiction is by no means the only source of blockbuster films, of course. But it is ideally suited to the needs of the blockbuster, precisely because it has so much potential for the production of expensive spectacular entertainment that can be exploited through a succession of different media. In other words, science fiction is located at a strategic point that fits perfectly into the New Hollywood corporate universe, and this is a major factor in the prominence of the genre. Science fiction is also found in independent or semi-independent films from America and elsewhere; in works such as *The Brother From Another Planet*, *Born in Flames*, *Repo Man* (1984) or the science fiction/horror hybrids directed by David Cronenberg. The dominant industrial landscape today often incorporates these potentially alternative channels. Independent or overseas science fiction is dependent on the major corporations some-times for finance and very often for distribution if it aspires to reach anything other than a very small audience. Hollywood can profit through this relationship by gaining access to sources of fresh ideas or approaches. The weird blends of the organic and inorganic explored in some of Cronenberg's films, for example, seem to have found their way into more mainstream examples including his own remake of *The Fly*. Hollywood's blockbuster science fiction is generally 'safer' and more conventional than works produced on the economic fringes, but it has established the centrality of some of the features according to which the genre is defined, none less than the subject of the following section: special effects.

Special Effects

One of the most common criticisms of contemporary science fiction cinema is that it relies too heavily on special effects. The claim that it amounts to little more than a load of expensive and essentially 'empty' special effects has already been dealt with implicitly by the first section of this book. We have shown that this is far from the case, given the number of substantial themes explored within the genre. There is more to the most effects-laden science fiction blockbuster than merely a hundred-million-dollar display of industrial fireworks. Special effects are important, however, and they often act as a key marker of the genre. Overt displays of effects are one of the defining characteristics of science fiction and an important draw for audiences. They are also a significant economic weapon for Hollywood, few others being able to afford to compete at the expensive high end of the latest effects technologies. They may not be all that matters in science fiction cinema, but flashy special effects are more than just an expensive form of icing on the cake.

What exactly is the appeal of special effects in science fiction films? The dominant tradition of writing about special effects has tended to be of the 'how did they do that' variety, or has concentrated on historical and technological descriptions of the various processes used, from the crudest work with models and back-projections to the latest wizardry of *computer-generated effects** (see, for example, Smith 1991; Vaz 1996). This is understandable up to a point. A sizeable part of the audience for books or articles on the subject is comprised of individuals seeking a better understanding of how the trickery works, the 'secrets' of the special effects conjurers. This is an interesting phenomenon and opens up questions about the ways special effects are experienced. They offer the possibility of 'representing the unrepresentable', showing things we can otherwise only imagine; realising our dreams and nightmares (with varying degrees of success). They are partly just about being 'amazed', but this is not a simple issue.

There is an essential tension in the way we consume special effects. An important dimension of anything considered to be a 'good' special effect is that it enables us to take it for a reality of some kind – to 'suspend disbelief', as the phrase goes, to enable us to put to the back of our minds for the moment the fact that we are watching a product of special effects. The classical marker of a 'bad' special effect is that we are reminded of its illusory status: if the wires are visible, the *blue or green screen** bleeds into the image or the models are just too obviously cardboard (although this can have its own appeal, as witnessed by the cult status of cheesy low-tech science fictions from *Attack of the Crab Monsters* to the homage paid in *Mars Attacks!*). But there is more to it than this. The perfect special effect, according to this version, would be invisible, seamlessly integrated into the action. An often-quoted example is the apparent failure of many viewers to realise that the ape creatures in the first section of *2001: A Space Odyssey* were not real but creations of costume and make-up effects.

The function of special effects, according to this view, is to serve narrative purposes, to make possible the images called for by the narrative, as Brooks Landon (1992) puts it. A story set on a fantastic imaginary planet needs effects that can create compelling images of a strange terrain; terrifying or wonderful aliens make similar demands on the special effects department. Better effects, seen this way, make the narrative more effective. They are particularly important in science fiction, a genre so often founded on the realisation of things that do not exist or are unknown or impossible at the time. An example of this way of understanding effects is provided by the two versions of *The Thing* (see Neale 1990; Landon 1992). In the novella on which the two films are based – 'Who Goes There?' by John Campbell (1938) – the alien is described in quite disturbing terms as a shape-shifting creature. Special effects were not capable of reproducing this kind of entity in 1951, so *The Thing* gives us its rather less terrifying creation, a humanoid vegetable memorably described by one character as an 'intellectual carrot'. When the story was filmed again in 1982 special effects techniques had developed to the point where it was possible to show something closer to the conception of the original story: a series of slimy and unpleasant organic transformations. Some criticised the remake for being dominated by its special effects, or for existing only for the purpose of unleashing such a spectacle. But, as Landon suggests, the effects are strongly led by the source narrative. The demands of the original narrative are more fully met by the achievements of improvements in special effects. But is this how we experience special effects, simply as servants of narrative? Or is our knowledge that they *are* effects an important aspect of that experience?

Special effects may claim our attention in their own right, rather than being subordinated to the demands of narrative. This is a common complaint among critics of contemporary science fiction cinema. Special effects are seen as interrupting or drawing our attention away from the story. Effects sequences are often described as 'bracketed-off' from the narrative (see Pierson 1999). Analysis of how this process works is often mixed up with value judgements: greater cultural worth tends to be attributed to narrative than to the pleasures provided by special effects. There may even be a class basis to such judgements, as Pierre Bourdieu (1986) suggests in his classic work on the cultural politics of 'taste'. Popular cultural products tend to offer an 'instant' and spectacular gratification sought by those who have little time to develop an affinity for more 'complex' works. The middle or upper classes mark themselves off as distinct from the lower classes by consuming works that enable them to show off their *cultural capital**. This may be one of the grounds on which science fiction cinema has often been found lacking in comparison with science fiction literature, which is often perceived as more 'intellectual', a judgement that tends to ignore the existence of vast quantities of pulp literature, particularly in America (see James 1994).

The appeal of special effects is undoubtedly one of the attractions offered by science fiction cinema, whether as a way of making convincing a fantastic narrative or providing audio-visual sensation for its own sake. It may be that our enjoyment lies precisely in the combination of these two kinds of experience: the pleasure of enjoying an awareness of the *process* of the illusion in which we partake (see La Valley 1985; for consideration of this issue in relation to an audience study, see Barker and Brooks 1998). This is a pleasure that may be at its peak when the effects are highly 'convincing'; when we are able to stand back just far enough from being entirely absorbed to delight in both halves of the equation (for a psychoanalytic take on this dynamic, see Metz 1977). Precisely such a dual focus appears within the 1982 version of *The Thing*. 'You've got to be fucking kidding,' observes one of the characters after the creature performs one of its bizarre transformations. As Steve Neale (1990) suggests, this comment can be taken on two levels: as part of the fictional world on screen, but also as a comment on the nature of the cinematic special effects themselves. Further examples of the pleasures offered by this kind of experience are the scenes of destruction in *Independence Day*. We are able to experience the spectacle of New York and the White House being blown to smithereens in a convincing way, while knowing quite clearly that this is a sophisticated piece of artifice. We can enjoy the spectacular destruction of such hallowed landmarks, taking pleasure in what appears to be a highly detailed realism of images that we are unlikely ever to see in the real world. At the same time, we can enjoy the knowledge that this is not real, and that we are not so naïve as to be fooled; and, in case it matters to us, that such icons of Western democracy and power remain safely intact.

This dual pleasure in special effects certainly makes sense in terms of what has historically been offered by Hollywood. A key aim of the Hollywood style of film-making has been to make the process invisible. The whole system of *continuity editing** around which Hollywood and many other brands of popular cinema have been built is designed to project the viewer effortlessly into the space on screen, and to avoid drawing attention to the act of construction involved. At the same time, however, Hollywood and Hollywood-influenced production has also appealed to the dimension of spectacle – to a celebration of the ability of the medium to present all sorts of illusion, magic and wonder for our enjoyment. Cinema as a form of magic, in this sense, has a history as long as the medium itself and has been closely associated with science fiction as far back as the work of Méliès. One of the pleasures offered by special effects is that technological progress is displayed at the level of the film-making process itself, even in films like the Terminator series that explicitly question our reliance on technology (see Landon 1992).

This seems to be the case in a number of films that portray imagined versions of virtual reality or the world inside a computer, a subject to which we return at the end of this section. This approach was pioneered by *Tron* and followed by *The Lawnmower Man*, among others. The shiny computer-generated graphics characteristic of early computer-generated animation are showcased when *The Lawnmower Man*'s Job (Jeff Fahey) is uploaded into the computer network. During the 1980s and early 1990s it became possible to achieve more complex and realistic looking surfaces through the use of *texture mapping**. But the artificially soft, polished finish was more appropriate to a film like *The Lawnmower Man*, both as a 'realistic' approximation of the world inside a computer and as a source of flashy imagery sold for its appeal as special effect. Audience awareness of the existence of effects *as* effects, and as effects that are presented as ever-improving, appears to add to their appeal. We might gain pleasure, for example, from measuring the differences between the effects used in the first *Star Wars* film and those used in the 'updated' re-releases of 1997 or the latest episode. We can identify with the latest and best versions, enabling us to look back at earlier versions from a position of superiority or fond nostalgia. None of these reactions are guaranteed, however, the *Star Wars* reissues and *The Phantom Menace* both having been criticised by some fans for relying on digital effects deemed to look 'phoney'.

Today's science fiction cinema is able to work on both levels of what is offered by special effects. Most mainstream films obey the usual rules of 'invisible' continuity editing and present us with story worlds into which we are invited to enter, to enjoy the dynamics of plot and of underlying narrative themes. They also offer special effects extravaganzas capable of being enjoyed in their own right and that remind us of the 'magical' capacities of the medium. This is pleasurable for audiences, seeking to temporarily escape the banality of the everyday, and helps to ensure the commercial success of the industry by staking its claim to offer effects that are truly 'special'. The impression does not always last. Each new generation of special effects is threatened by the prospect of future developments that will leave them looking dated and unconvincing. With some notable exceptions such as the evergreen *2001*, special effects come with their own sell-by dates, another factor that helps Hollywood to promote our continued consumption of new science fictions. Always, around the corner, is the promise of a wave of still better effects technologies that will wow audiences afresh and lure us back, repeatedly, to the movie theatre – or to spend our money on expensive domestic products that claim to offer a replication of something like the cinematic experience.

'Sounds weird': Music and Sound in Science Fiction Cinema

If the future, space or aliens look spectacular, they can also sound strangely different. Sound effects, music and even silence are important factors in science fiction: they are often crucial to its dramatic and emotional impact. Sound is a dimension frequently neglected by analysis, although the film industry, both past and present, has invested in the development of audio technologies that increase its ability to convey a sense of wonder or otherness. During the rise of science fiction as a staple genre in 1950s Hollywood, new electronic instruments were used in conjunction with images of aliens landing on Earth, to create an aura of strangeness. *Forbidden Planet* was one of the first films to rely primarily on electronically produced sound. One particular instrument associated with 1950s science fiction is the theremin, invented by Lev Theremin in the early 1920s. Its eerie wailing glissando seems to capture a sense of other-wordliness and was often used to accompany the presence of aliens, as in Bernard Herrman's score for *The Day the Earth Stood Still*. The use of the theremin more recently in *Mars Attacks!* is an important aspect of the film's effort to evoke the character of 1950s science fiction.

The coldness or abstract nature of electronically produced sound is often used to represent the non-human. *Planet of the Vampires* (1965) makes use of *non-pitched synthesised sound** to evoke the hostility and unfamiliarity of outer space. This can be contrasted to the warmer and more organic tones of the conventional orchestra, used to connote the emotional world of humanity, a device used in *Flight to Mars*. *Zardoz* deploys random, low-end chords to aurally underpin the barbarity of the *homo sapien* outlanders. Beethoven and medieval-style songs are aligned with the God-like, but ultimately more decadent, 'eternals'. The original *Invasion of the Body Snatchers* organises its use of music around a different kind of opposition. *Non-diegetic music** is generally used to heighten suspense and to maintain the fast pace of the action. *Diegetic music** from a jukebox and the radio is used, alternatively, in brief moments of respite. Exactly what these different kinds of music signify is used to mislead the two principal protagonists, Miles Bennel (Kevin McCarthy) and Becky Driscoll (Dana Wynter), when they hole up in a cave, exhausted from their flight from the 'pod-people'. Through the darkness they hear the strains of a gentle love song: they rejoice, believing that only real humans could produce such an expression, but it turns out to be just a song playing on the 'pod' farmer's car radio.

Some recent science fiction cinema uses contemporary popular music as part of its strategy to attract a youth audience. *Tank Girl* draws on the work of contemporary 'indie' bands, with extracts from songs by Portishead and Hole providing direct reference to feisty female singers who might stand comparison with the central character. The film exploits the cultural capital associated with the music to appeal to a 'hip' teenage and twenty-something audience. The music is heavily foregrounded, often giving the film the appearance of a series of MTV videos stitched around the protagonist's anti-establishment adventures. This is very different from the use of music in *2001*, which broke new ground in the way it used classical themes in a science fiction context. The challenging *avant garde atonal** work of György Ligeti (*Atmospheres* (1961) and *Lux aeterna*, (1966)) contributes greatly to the film's evocation of infinite space and time. This is set against the tonal familiarity and grandeur of Richard Strauss's *Also Sprach Zarathustra* (1896). The use of these classical pieces contributes to the film's own status as a 'classic' rather than a film that appears outdated more than thirty years after its release (*2001* also makes striking use of silence in some key sequences). Another example of the use of atonal music is the opening scene of *Planet of the Apes* (1968) where it helps to create an impression of strangeness on the planet reached by the astronaut George Taylor (Charlton Heston) and his crew.

Atonal music is found relatively rarely. Science fiction, like other films, reverts generally to more familiar and conventional strains to underpin the dynamics of the narrative. Dissonance might be used in moments of tension, while more melodic themes characterise periods of repose. The contrast between the two contributes significantly to textual richness, despite the formulaic nature of much film music. Like other films, science fiction uses music to create atmosphere and to provide contexts for the viewer to read beyond what is directly represented on screen. But sound is not simply a textual event, as we have seen. Like most ingredients of science fiction, it plays a role in attracting particular audience groups. It is also an important aspect of the corporate strategy of contemporary global media industry giants, most of which have stakes in the recording industry. The music foregrounded in films is often owned by record labels belonging to the same corporate group as the company involved in the production, finance and/or distribution of the movie. This integrated system enables films to market themselves through the record industry, and vice-versa. The theme tune for *Men in Black* sung by Will Smith made it into the singles charts, opening up a further marketing route through MTV and radio: Will Smith was signed to Columbia records, owned by Sony, and the film was made by Sony Pictures and Columbia.

Explosions, rocket engines, sounds of data being processed: space may in reality be silent to the human ear, but in science fiction it can be extremely noisy. Sound effects play a crucial role in the spectacular impact of contemporary science fiction. In some cases, the sound of science fiction is subordinated to or less exciting than the visuals. Dialogue often verges on the banal to establish an aesthetic of authenticity, as in 1950s films such as *Destination Moon*. It is also used widely as a way of explaining what is going on, or as a point of contrast to fantastic imagery. *2001* again offers vivid illustration, the sparseness of dialogue reflecting what the film presents as a waning of humanity in the face of technology and cosmic forces. Sound effects are often used more emphatically today, to heighten excitement and create a physical impact on the body of the viewer. In *Contact* the alien intelligence is signified almost entirely by loud pulsating sounds, akin to those of a gigantic heartbeat, picked up from outer space. Sometimes, as in *Lost in Space*, sound effects become so loud as to obscure our ability to hear some of the dialogue. *Alien* presents us with awesome and terrifying images, but it also relies heavily on sound effects to startle us. Sub-sonic rumbles are often less heard than felt bodily, a celebrated example being the opening of *Star Wars*.

The success of these audio strategies is dependent on the ability of sound systems to create multi-spatial sounds, to open up the cinema auditorium to sound coming from every direction and textured in multiple layers. Audiences and owners of cinema chains have, historically, been relatively slow to invest in the benefits of superior sound systems, a situation that appears to have begun to change in recent years. The potential of 'big sound', to go with the 'big picture', has been recognised by Hollywood as another way to stress the specific qualities offered by the cinematic experience. The multi-channel cinema sound system offers far more aural impact than two-channel television, and even the more sophisticated home systems remain constrained by the volume limits imposed by a domestic setting. George Lucas invested considerably in his THX sound system, a variation on Dolby Surround Sound, and much has been made of his apparent reluctance to allow cinemas not equipped with this system to have access to much sought-after prints of *The Phantom Menace*. Overall, the provision of sound impact is another dimension of the contemporary blockbuster phenomenon to which science fiction is well suited.

Shaping Things to Come: the Design of Science Fiction

Lurex, latex and leather; alien planets, space-age cityscapes and classically streamlined flying saucers: the spectacular impact of science fiction cinema is dependent not only on special effects technologies, but also the work of set and costume designers. They make a major contribution to the impact and pleasure of the genre, although these aspects of science fiction cinema – particularly costume design – often come in for less sustained analysis than seemingly more serious narrative themes. For many viewers it is precisely the look or style of a film that is enjoyable, although design does not only contribute to the spectacular dimension, as it is often closely associated with narrative themes and issues. Design styles are usually a good indicator of the period in which a film is made: *Flash Gordon* has the imprint of the 1930s, *Forbidden Planet* is instantly locatable in the 1950s, the costumes of *Logan's Run* are recognisably 1970s while the shapes and special effects of *Starship Troopers* are unmistakably 1990s. Most science fiction films tend to fall into a limited set of broad design styles which might be defined approximately as: futurism, retro-futurism, realism, gothic and post-apocalyptic.

Most viewers of *Metropolis* will be struck by the detailed landscape of the *expressionist** set and costumes that locate it within the avant-garde aesthetics of the early twentieth century. The film established in many ways the school of cine-futurism, which has its roots partly in the Italian-based *futurist** movement, but is more than simply an obsession with speed and technological progress. The film's labyrinth of skyscrapers, factories and stairways leading nowhere blend visions of the fantastic with the director Fritz Lang's fascination with the contemporary Manhattan skyline. The design is not mere decoration but central to the film's critique of the alienating and inhuman qualities of capitalism.

The vertiginous high-rise landscapes of *Metropolis* set a precedent for many followers, including *Things to Come* and the polymorphous architectural design of *Blade Runner*. The retro-futurist production style of *Blade Runner* appears to be a major aspect of the appeal of the film, a legacy taken up in the teeming cityscapes of *Judge Dredd*, *The Fifth Element* (1997) and *Dark City* (1997). *Blade Runner* has been described as almost losing itself in its dedication to extremely fine detail, much of which is impossible to fully grasp even on repeated viewings; parking meters on the main street set, for example, included fine-print warnings of the danger of lethal electric shock faced by anyone tampering with the mechanism (see Sammon 1996). But the design of the city is central to political aspects of the film. The elite live in penthouses high above the accumulated trash and low-life rabble of the streets. The chief replicant Roy Batty (Rutger Hauer) transgresses this spatial and social boundary as he ascends a vast pyramidal structure to confront and kill his maker.

In the 1950s most science fiction was shot in black and white. The effects are usually cheap and most of the films have little pretension to more than B-movie status. They tend to pursue a generally realistic aesthetic, however, as do the few colour examples of the period such as *Destination Moon*, *Flight to Mars* and *War of the Worlds*. Framed within what is presented as an everyday, contemporary setting, the futurist dimension of 1950s science fiction is often located in the design of the alien spaceship and its inhabitants. It is something brought to us from elsewhere. A greater presence of futuristic design is more likely to be

FIGURE 6 *Metropolis (1927)*

found in films of the period in which we are taken to other worlds. In *Forbidden Planet*, for example, it seems significant that the NASA crew reach Altair IV in a classically-styled flying saucer of the kind usually associated with alien visitors to Earth. The futuristic environment becomes something that can be occupied by ordinary humanity as its scope is extended to the domestic realm. The house of Morbius on Altair IV is a celebration of a 1950s design ideal. Glass and steel form the main structural components in conjunction with clean-lined utilitarian furniture and exotic plants, the shapes of which form part of the interior architecture. The futuristic design and its technologies are an extrapolation from contemporary developments and aspirations. In this respect it is rather like Morbius himself, an 'ordinary' mortal rooted in the world of his own culture who was able to create the dwelling and its wonders after using an alien Krel device to expand the capacity of his brain. The design of the film establishes a juxtaposition between homely, recognisable versions of the future and more radical visions: the dream-house sits above vast abyssal structures of Krel technology that stretch towards an unsettling and vertiginous vision of the infinite.

The utopian aspect of the 1950s ideal home in *Forbidden Planet* is completed by its setting in an Edenic garden complete with limpid pool and tame wild animals. This is further reflected in the use of costume to underpin character. Altaira's skimpy clothes – and their absence when she swims in the pool – suggest a pre-lapsarian innocence, threatened by her father's access to the 'forbidden fruit' of Krel technology. Morbius dresses mainly in black with an overcoat that could be a professor's robe or a magician's cape, intimating the dark and corrupting forces he inadvertently summons. The uniforms of the American visitors are utilitarian, partly based on contemporary naval uniforms but also referring back to the garb of 1930s science fiction in the use of shoulder pads and ribbing. Costume also reflects narrative themes in *Things to Come*, contributing to the film's equivocal stance on the value of science and rationality. John Cabal might at first be placed as a heroic figure, but he appears from the sky in black costume and an elongated helmet that give him the qualities of an alien, an appearance that prompts Boss to describe him as machine-like. Boss does not seem a very sympathetic character, yet wears garments made from fur over his warlord's uniform and bandoleers, giving him a more organic and 'primitive' appearance in keeping with his claims about the threat science poses to nature.

In a recycling process typical of the genre, the sets and male costumes of *Forbidden Planet* were used again in the splendidly kitsch *Queen of Outer Space*, in which the all-women Venusians are decked out in mini skirts and high heels. Both *Forbidden Planet* and *Queen of Outer Space* look back to the campy futurism of the *Flash Gordon* serials of the 1930s in which the space hero is done up in a tight-fitting jumpsuit and women wear skimpy costumes and diaphanous chiffon. Women's costumes in science fiction cinema are not only physically revealing, but also often blatantly fetishistic. The black leather dominatrix look is a key visual feature of *Devil Girl From Mars* (1954) and evident in the costumes of the lesbian Black Queen (Anita Pallenberg) and her acolytes in the modish comic-book style fantasy *Barbarella*. The sleek skin-tight black leather/ PVC outfits worn by Trinity in *The Matrix* provides a more recent example of fetishistic attire.

A recreation of the look of classic B-movie science fiction is found in *Mars Attacks!*, a film inspired by the design of a series of bubble-gum cards produced in 1962 and based on films such as *This Island Earth*, *Invaders from Mars* (1953) and *Invasion of the Saucer Men*. The costume and production design are both inspired by and parody the 1950s look. *Mars Attacks!* takes the *Blade Runner* principle of hybrid design to a pitch of hyper-stylised trash aesthetics, especially in the scenes set in Las Vegas: cowboy rhinestones meets *I Dream of Jeannie* (1965–1970) (the pseudo-Arabian clothes of the 1960s series given a 'New Age' make-over) and even the aliens wear lurex capes. At an opposite extreme, *THX 1138*, an early film directed by George Lucas, figures its dystopian future in terms of stark, minimalist images. The characters are at times reduced to dark silhouettes picked out against a blinding white background suggestive of a sterile, undifferentiated world in which individuality and love are suppressed. The central characters are imprisoned in doorways and other divisions within the frame in compositions sometimes verging on the abstract; design and camerawork pushes them to the very edge of the screen to indicate the extent to which human intimacy has been marginalised.

Cold and sparse design also supports the narrative themes of the more recent *Gattaca*, which draws on the *Bauhaus** style in its furniture and buildings. *Gattaca* uses this style as a form of retro-futurism. It is present in the corporate look of the Gattaca campus and echoed in the house of Jerome Morrow (Jude Law). The film deploys a distinctive colour scheme. Golden shades, usually associated with the glow of human warmth, are used widely but burnished surfaces render them muted and toned, in accordance with the passivity that dominates this world of genetic determinism. Business suits and sleek hairstyles further emphasise a thematic concern with tidy perfectionism and controlled environment. The Bauhaus movement was disbanded by the Nazi regime in Germany, but the film's theme of oppressive genetic determinism suggests that the style offers tacit reference to Nazi experiments in eugenics.

The dystopian austerity of *THX 1138* and *Gattaca* contrasts with the lush Irish landscapes used to suggest a post-apocalyptic return to pre-industrial agrarian life, of various kinds, in *Zardoz*. *Zardoz* and *Planet of the Apes* mark a shift in science fiction design, away from the pristine futurist look that had been used to suggest both utopian and dystopian qualities. The bleak post-apocalyptic landscapes of the *Mad Max* trilogy (1979, 1981, 1985), *Hardware* (1990), *Waterworld* and *Tank Girl* are littered with the rusting carcasses of beached technologies and costume designs are derived from biker leathers, hippy and punk styles. There is no question here of figuring the future in terms of progress or gleaming new designs. That kind of world has been destroyed, leaving only its debris. What is left is a mixture of barbarism, nomadism and opportunistic scavenging in the hi-tech scrap-heap.

The design of the futuristic often entails the creation of a cold, clinical and alienating environment, in keeping with the thematic concerns of the genre. It is contrasted to the softness, cosiness, mess or diverse colours of more 'human' domestic spaces. It is easy to forget that the contemporary domestic setting is designed at all, its world being so familiar from representations if not always from reality. Take a science fiction film like *E.T.*, for example. The work of design is most obviously foregrounded in the look of the spaceship and E.T. itself. The suburban domestic setting in which the bulk of the action occurs is likely to be taken for granted. In some ways, though, it is just as much a rhetorical landscape as that of any imaginary alien planet: a world of material richness and clutter, soft toys and squabbles. This is not presented as entirely unproblematic – a major subtext of the film is the issue of the absent father – but it is, ultimately, a celebration of a particular fantasy of late twentieth-century American life.

In *The Lawnmower Man* most of the action takes places in two contrasting spaces: the house of Dr Angelo and the corporate environment in which he is employed. Angelo's house is 'lived-in', inhabited in a human manner. Used food cartons litter a basement den equipped with comfortable reclining chairs. His bedroom is a mess; he smokes and

FIGURE 7 *Tank Girl (1995)*

watches television in bed, much to his wife's chagrin. The technology he uses at home is shrouded in a tangle of wires and squeezed into a small space, unlike the sleek work environment at Virtual Space Industries. The sinister corporate space is secure, windowless and forbidding. Virtual reality experiments are conducted in a large gyroscopic assemblage in which the subject is restrained by straps, quite unlike the relaxed 'floating' position adopted in Angelo's domestic rig. The technologies and gadgets of the sympathetic scientist are softened by their location in the domestic design environment, although, in the case of *The Lawnmower Man*, this also creates tension. Technology might gain a more human edge, but it also threatens the integrity of the home. Angelo's wife soon walks out in frustration at the amount of time he spends immersed in the virtual worlds accessible in the basement; a similar fate befalls the eccentric Professor Wayne Szalinski (Rick Moranis) in *Honey, I Shrunk the Kids*.

Many science fiction films move between the utopian and dystopian presentation of their future worlds, another aspect of the genre in which design plays a central part. *Things to Come* and *Starship Troopers* may be more than half a century apart, but they share a similar futuristic design. Both the college campus in the early scenes of *Starship Troopers* and the future buildings of *Things to Come* are airy constructions in white and glass, exhibiting the features of Bauhaus style. Clean, clear and uncluttered structures are meant to privilege the human dimension. Spaces are established for dialogue and democratic interaction according to the principle that the atrium is a kind of classical Greek *agora*, the market-place to which citizens came to discuss issues and vote. What is commonly asserted by these apparently bright and open spaces is a false version, the proclaimed utopia that is in fact an oppressive (or potentially oppressive) society that denies human individuality and idiosyncrasy. *Starship Troopers* adopts a rather mixed approach here. It presents a version of democracy quite unusual in that it follows the literal Greek definition, according to which only those with the status of 'citizens' have the right to vote. The film has plenty of satirical bite, yet does not present much to indicate the oppression of the disenfranchised. It also establishes a nostalgia for its version of Buenos Aires, established as the home city of the central characters, whether considered utopian or not, after it is atomised by alien attack.

If the inviting spaces of would-be utopias are meant to promote at least a façade of democracy and openness, many science fiction films offer an obscure and convoluted design principle that reflects still darker thematic concerns. The *Alien* films, *Event Horizon*, *Dune* (1984) and *Brazil* (1985) figure the future in terms of the *gothic**. *Dune* is in many ways a classic gothic narrative of the fight between good and evil. Its embellished style is mirrored in a convoluted plot involving the fight for freedom, telepathy, tortures and rites of passage. The future meets the Victorian gothic in the design of devices such as the ornamented wood and curved glass tank in which the giant embryo-like Supreme Being is housed, a structure Vivian Sobchack describes as like an 'old museum display case' (1993: 278). Many of the costumes are modelled on the styles of late nineteenth- and early twentieth-century Europe, including military uniforms and waist-clinching Victorian and Edwardian-style dresses. Hooked up to intravenous tubing and bearing suppurating sores as badges of his unpleasant office, the evil Baron Harkonnen (Kenneth McMillan) is an excessive gothic monster who pleasures himself through gratuitous and abject acts that involve consuming the body parts or fluids of his victims. *Dune's* heavy gothic styles, derived from a host of historical periods, are married to the hallucinatory effects of the opium-like *melange* taken by the central character, a name that could equally refer to the delirious amalgamation of visual styles used in the film. *Brazil* also deploys aspects of the gothic to present its version of alienating dystopia, producing a grotesque style typical of the work of its director, Terry Gilliam. *Brazil* is a blend of the gothic and the retro-futurist, often drawing on *surrealism** in its dark and bizarre images. Echoing Franz Kafka's nightmare vision of labyrinthine and inexplicable bureaucracy, the decrepit building where the central character Sam Lowry (Jonathan Pryce) lives is a complex knot of ducts and wires that takes on almost organic qualities.

Gothic qualities are also found in the *Alien* films, which exhibit some startling designs. The alien, the work of the Swiss artist H. R. Giger, is one of the most strange and terrifying creations of the entire genre. Giger's eerie set designs for the first film combine the polished gun-metal grey tones of technology with the organic shapes of gigantic fossilised bones. The sleek lines of the alien's steely domed head, its metallic teeth and acid blood suggest something purely mechanical. It grows, however, from an egg-like structure and goes through an early stage as a rather repulsively organic, tentacled creature known as the 'face-hugger'. The giant alien spacecraft explored by the main characters displays a similar mixture of the technological and the seemingly organic. As a number of critics have suggested, the film appears to displace some of its concern with issues of gender onto this kind of production design, particularly a fear of a monstrous version of the feminine (see Creed 1993). The characterisation of Ripley might represent a feminist fantasy of sexual equality, signified, partly, by costume: Ripley wears the same work overalls as the rest of the crew, male and female, although much debate has focused on the significance of the climactic scene, before which she strips to her underclothes. If this is the case, Judith Newton (1990) suggests, the alien, and the milieu it occupies, might represent male hostility and anxiety about the gains of feminism. The alien spacecraft is entered through an opening that has been interpreted as vaginal, situated between the two open 'legs' of the ship's structure. The alien itself has phallic qualities, particularly in the shape of its head, but can also be seen from a psychoanalytical perspective as an archaic image of castration anxiety (see, again, Creed 1993).

The alien spacecraft need not be seen solely as a figuration of the female body. It suggests, more generally, a disturbing conflation of the technological and the organic, creating a compelling setting within which the human figure is dwarfed; an image that draws from the classical gothic idea of the awesome and inhuman scale of the sublime. If the alien vessel takes on the dark unfathomable qualities of the gothic, so does the Nostromo, the ship occupied by the film's protagonists. This is no shiny or redundantly aerodynamic construction like the classic flying saucers or rockets of the 1950s and their imitators. From the outside, it is a clumsy dark structure befitting its role as a mundane cargo-hauler. Inside, with its ducts, passages and dripping holds, it shares the organic bowel-like qualities of its alien equivalent. The spaceship of *Event Horizon* and the vertiginous fractal complexity of the Borg ships in *Star Trek: First Contact* follow the gothic character of the ships in *Alien*, their design reflecting the malignant terrors awaiting boarders.

While the gothic style tends to rely on darkness to evoke the strange terrors of alien worlds, other films use light to construct the extraordinary or intangible. The association between light and truth is recurrent in science fiction. The beams of powerful torches penetrating the mysterious darkness are a characteristic design feature of *The X Files*. Mulder and Scully's torches signify their quest for the truth of many beguiling phenomena. Light does not always suggest enlightenment, however. The light-flooded spaces of utopia often conceal the darker shadows of totalitarianism, as we have seen. The UFOs of *Close Encounters* give off a blinding light that at first seems threatening, as well as contributing to the cinematic spectacle. Light, in varying colours, is a key design ingredient of the film: the spaceships consist of little else, in fact, a major element of what is meant to be a dazzling experience for protagonists and cinema-goers.

Set design and costume offer additional resources in the battle for a distinct identity or marketing line among the procession of contemporary science fiction blockbusters. *The Fifth Element* found its angle by signing up Jean-Paul Gaultier, the *enfant terrible* of the fashion world. His costumes manifest a version of retro-futurism that embraces a camp perspective on the styles found in *Barbarella* and the Flash Gordon series: the evil Jean Baptiste Emmanuel Zorg (Gary Oldman) is decked out in a costume not dissimilar to that worn by Ming the Merciless. *The Fifth Element* joins other science fiction films such as *Dune*, *The City of Lost Children* and *Lost in Space* that have sometimes been accused of offering an excess of design at the expense of content, in much the same way as many are taken to task for their reliance on special effects. A similar response might be offered in reply: extraordinary design, like extravagant effects, can in itself be a major appeal and a defining feature of the genre for both industry and audiences alike.

Robots and Rayguns: Computers, Gadgets and Gizmos

Clunky switches, dials and control panels are instant signifiers of what retrospectively appears to be the low-tech design of 1950s science fiction. At the opposite extreme, the computer graphics of *Johnny Mnemonic* present a deliriously hi-tech interface in which the title character at a desk can lay virtual hands directly onto vast landscapes of cyberspace data. The design of science fiction films is not limited to the grand vistas of alien landscapes, future architectures or spacecraft, but also entails the imagination of a host of other technological devices. These range from the large and narratively central – weapons, computers and robots, for example – to the smaller detail, the gadgets and gizmos that are often among the most memorable features of projected other worlds.

The design of robots and computers often reflects their ability to stand as loyal servants or dangerous enemies. The Michelin-man-type curves of Robby the robot in *Forbidden Planet* suggest endearing and almost cuddly characteristics. Robby is a nurturing figure, with a stomach compartment that delivers endless quantities of food or drink. Caring for, or looked

FIGURE 8 *Barbarella (1968)*

after by, young boys in *The Invisible Boy* (1957) and the television series *Lost in Space* (1965–1968), Robby is the first in a line of cute droids, such as R2D2 (*Star Wars*), Huey, Dewey and Louie (*Silent Running*) and Johnny 5 (*Short Circuit*, 1986). The perspex dome of Robby's head is transparent, enabling us to see into some of his inner workings. In contrast, the visage of the cyclopean Gort in *The Day the Earth Stood Still* is inscrutable, its visor opening only to fire deadly rays. Gort is silent, impervious to human communication, its metallic skin resisting any earthly drill. Gort's legacy is apparent in a range of hostile robots, although attitude does not always follow appearance quite so clearly. The series ED209 law-enforcement droid unveiled at the start of *RoboCop* is presented as part of the forces of corporate evil, as well as being somewhat crazed and out of control. Its menacing broad-shouldered design is echoed by that of Robot in the film version of *Lost in Space*, but Robot is presented quite clearly as a technology whose behaviour depends on its programming. Sabotaged early on with instructions to destroy the Robinson family, Robot is a fearsome monster; reprogrammed, it comes closer to the role model set by Robby and is subject to the benign control of the schoolboy Will Robinson (Jack Johnson).

The computer comes in many different guises. Sometimes it is given human characteristics, usually a voice. In other cases the computer is simply a boxed interface providing data that remains invisible. In *Quatermass and the Pit* a large computer is wheeled in to make visible the hallucinations experienced by those who have come into contact with the Martians. Fed by a helmet studded with electrodes, the computer's spool heads whirr away to project subjective images onto a small domestic television set. In some films the computer becomes a central protagonist in the action. The HAL 9000 of *2001* is one of the most noted examples, especially as it seems to exhibit more 'human' qualities than the members of the crew. HAL speaks in soft, slow reassuring tones, but possesses a gleaming, all-seeing red eye that takes on sinister connotations. Unusually, *2001* takes us inside the computer's workings: a sparse red-lit chamber in which its higher functions are represented by the lines of simple box-like circuits (disconnected in an impromptu lobotomy performed by the astronaut Dave Bowman (Keir Dullea)). Computers also play major roles in *Dark Star* and *Demon Seed* (where Proteus IV is voiced in smoothly menacing tones by Robert Vaughan), but it is more common for them to exist as part of the background techno-infrastructure, as in the *Star Trek* series.

Alien or futuristic spacecraft are often filled with devices or equipment that serve rhetorical purposes rather than being clearly explained or highlighted by the action. They assert 'futuristic', 'alien' or 'advanced' without offering any literal account of what exactly they do or how they work. Their meaning lies precisely in being taken for granted as part of the texture of other worlds. Navigation devices offer further examples. *Forbidden Planet* has a transparent spherical structure to which the attentions of the flying saucer pilot and crew are turned during manoeuvres, although its precise function is not made clear. A similar feature is found on the flight deck of the alien saucers of *This Island Earth*: an open framework sphere that could be a model either of a planetary system or a complex atomic structure, either of which would be relevant to the narrative material of the film. A more up to date version, from the perspective of the imagination and special effects of the 1990s, is the whirling 3D holographic navigation device on the Jupiter 2 spacecraft of *Lost in Space*.

Circles and spheres such as these are key images in the overall design of science fiction. They are the shapes of planets, galaxies and, of course, the classic flying saucer. The entire fabric of space and time are 'curved' in the visions of some films, a characteristic that permits science fiction much of its narrative range: warp drives, worm-holes, circular gateways to other dimensions and temporal loops give wide latitude to the science fiction imagination. The circle or sphere also signifies a more general sense of technology or rationality. The giant revolving space station of *2001* reminds us of the wheel, often viewed as one of the most important early technologies, an association that hardly seems accidental in a film that opens with a depiction of the introduction of humans to the use of technology. The sphere is a shape that seems to reflect the world of nature, in the form of planets and suns, or more ancient beliefs and imagined cosmologies. Locanio (1987) offers a reading of such science fiction cinema iconography in terms of the circular mandala symbol of harmonious totality in Carl Jung's theory of archetypes. Real heavenly bodies are not perfect spheres, however: the ideal sphere is an image of engineered or mathematical perfection, a signifier of pure rationality. Fantastic possibilities are unleashed by the glowing sphere brought to present-day earth by a time-travelling spaceship in *Sphere* (1998). The rational is mixed here with the irrational, an ambiguity we have witnessed elsewhere in the genre: the powers of this spherical entity include a capacity to make real the worst nightmares of the characters.

If the perfect sphere can be a signifier of rationality in the design of science fiction, so might other geometric shapes. The other-worldliness of Proteus IV in *Demon Seed* is signified partly in the swirling designs that appear on the monitor screens of the artificial intelligence, but also in the weird and threatening polygonal structure it creates in the basement of the Harris house. The principal signifier of the superior alien intelligence of *2001* is the famous black monolith that appears at key moments in the narrative, a matt surface of impenetrable and inscrutable abstract purity. The protagonists of *Cube* are imprisoned within a labyrinthine geometric structure resembling a giant Rubik's cube. Each character has a theory about the origins of the structure but no definitive explanation is provided. The cube, like *2001*'s monolith, remains enigmatic, supplying an appropriate setting for a claustrophobic psychodrama. Only the solution to its mathematical puzzle leads to the way out: a case of rationality as both design principle and plot resolution. An enormous cube is also a fitting design for the spaceship occupied by the coldly rational Borg of *Star Trek: First Contact*.

The zapping ray or laser beam weapon provides another of the quintessential images of science fiction. Bright beams fire across the screen with a familiarity equal to that the western's six-gun. Alien invaders fire rays that, in classic style, vaporise or explode human bodies and equipment, as in *Earth vs. the Flying Saucers* (1956). That conventional weapons are useless in response is a familiar cliché; aliens usually come equipped with personalised defensive force-fields. Human ingenuity finds a response, of course. In *Earth vs. the Flying Saucers* this comes in the form of a device to disrupt the magnetic fields used by the alien craft, a glorious example of the 1950s futuristic aesthetic that resembles a giant raygun mounted on the back of a truck. In *Independence Day*, where the alien death ray creates massive and spectacular destruction, a fatal computer virus does the job. From the chunky rayguns of early science fiction to the blasters and lightsabers of the *Star Wars* series, futuristic weapons often create an impression of warfare that is clean and clinical, undoubtedly part of the motivation for the adoption of the term 'Star Wars' for the Reagan administration's Strategic Defensive Initiative.

A multitude of handy gizmos and gadgets turn up in science fiction. Many are small and play no significant narrative role, but they remain important to the overall *mise-en-scène*. Prosthetic devices to augment human vision offer one strain of examples. The glasses worn by Jedediah (Bruce Spence) in *Mad Max: Beyond Thunderdome* (1985) enhance his eccentric inventor appearance. Many recent science fictions furnish protagonists with sunglasses that are not futuristic in themselves but create an aura of futuristic cool and enigma, as in *The Matrix* and *Men in Black*. Geordi Le Forge (LeVar Burton) in *Star Trek: First Contact* has eyes that have the performance capability of a camera, including telescopic and infra-red functions. The Borg enemy in *First Contact* use prosthetic eye attachments that serve a variety of functions, not least to make them more menacing. Similar designs are worn by the blind child-catching cyclops-men in *The City of Lost Children*, devices that enable them to see, although these are made from brass in keeping with the Victorian gothic style of the film's technology.

The perspective of optical enhancement can also be offered to the viewer in the form of subjective point-of-view shots. *The Terminator* gives us a threatening cyber-view of the world as seen through an infra-red lens and accompanied by analytical data, an effect used in a more voyeuristic manner in *Hardware*, in which the robotic eye is conflated with that of a peeping tom. Similar effects are also found in *Westworld* (1973) and *RoboCop*. Extra visual powers are accorded to Deckard in *Blade Runner* through the Esper machine that enables him to explore the world inside photographs as if they were three-dimensional representations. Another handy device is the Voight-Kampf apparatus, a weird structure containing a lens and bellows, used to measure the emotional responses of those suspected of being replicants. The design of the Voight-Kampf machine makes some gesture to being understandable in terms of its function. We are told, for example, that pupil dilation is one of the responses being measured and we see this being examined through its lens. Many science fiction gadgets make no such efforts, however, and are often all the more fun for their fantastic claims. A short spike-ended object in *The Day the Earth Stood Still* would have enabled the American president to communicate with other worlds if it had not been damaged, announces the alien Klaatu, something we have to take purely on faith. A similar rhetoric accompanies the phallic-shaped silver gizmo with its flashing light used by 'K' (Tommy Lee Jones) in *Men in Black* to wipe the memories of unauthorised figures who come across the aliens living in their midst. The 'dilithium crystals' of *Star Trek*, a largely unexplained source of power, are one of the most cited examples of the kind of imaginary techno-jargon that accompanies such devices.

Gadgets designed to help with daily domestic life are supplied more rarely than weapons and industrial hardware, perhaps reflecting the traditionally assumed male-dominance of the genre. There are notable exceptions: Robby the robot does all the domestic duties in *Forbidden Planet*, the dream house which boasts a handy kitchen 'disintegrator' for waste disposal. Robby can synthesize anything, including food and drink that tastes just like the real thing, much to the delight of the cook who is presented with gallons of perfect hangover-free bourbon. The humanoid Martians of *Flight to Mars* have dispensed with domestic kitchens: food is delivered automatically to the home through a drawer mechanism and the washing up is 'taken care of mechanically', leading the 'lady scientist' Carol (Virginia Huston) to proclaim Mars a 'woman's paradise'. The home of the scientist in *Demon Seed* is also full of labour-saving devices. The occupants of some science fiction, however, are less fortunate in their dietary arrangements. The barrenness of space in *2001* is reflected on board in the food as much as anything else, reduced to a series of coloured pastes scraped or sucked from a future version of a TV-dinner tray. A similar kind of food is found in *Sleeper*, which also boasts an unappealing form of 'instant pudding' that swells to comically monstrous proportions. The post-apocalyptic world of *Hardware* has milk cartons that look familiar enough, unlike their content: 'lactoplasm'. Future foodstuffs can also take on greater thematic significance – for instance they are central to the narrative of *Soylent Green* (1973).

If nutrition is a fond subject for amusing detail in science fiction, it is hardly surprising that the concerns of the lower regions also feature. Sex has often been described as relatively absent from science fiction, which is true, partly because future technologies tend to offer sublimated versions, often played for laughs. An obviously comic example is the 'orgasmatron' of *Sleeper*, a cylindrical chamber that flashes red and green lights as it stimulates the occupant. Taking the sex machine into more fetishistic realms, *Barbarella* features an infernal pleasure/torture contraption: the 'excesses machine'. Played as an instrument by Duran Duran (Milo O'Shea), it has a number of long rubber tongues that undulate across the length of Barbarella's body. In the bland would-be-utopia of *Demolition Man* sex takes the form of a pair of metal skull-caps worn on the back of the head as the subjects sit several feet apart: rapidly-cut flashing images of the sexual partner characterise copulation by means of a 'digitised transfer of sexual energy', a practice deemed safer than physical contact in a world of post-AIDS sexually transmitted diseases. A further extreme is represented by the 'cyber-sex' of *The Lawnmower Man*, in which computer graphics versions of virtual reality bodies merge and blend in electronic ecstasy. Further, 'how do you go to the toilet' jokes are familiar fare from films about space travel. The moon shuttle traveller of *2001* is advised to carefully study the instructions before using the 'zero gravity toilet'. *Demolition Man* envisages a futuristic replacement for toilet paper. Three 'seashells' are used, a set of silver-coloured objects that sits next to the toilet bowl; exactly what is done with them is not explained, either to the viewer or the puzzled twentieth-century protagonist, John Spartan.

Science fiction films have produced many memorable designs, from the slickest futurism to the most dark and encrusted nightmare structures.

Radical difference is seldom attempted, however, a fact that some commentators find disappointing. However hard it tries to imagine weird and wonderful futures or other worlds, science fiction cinema rarely escapes entirely from the looks, any more than the thematic concerns, of its own historical periods and fashions. It is constrained partly by generic and financial limitations, but also by the demand to be comprehensible. Utter strangeness and difference might entail an abstract conception, impossible to grasp. This has been attempted in some cases – parts of the 'stargate' sequence of *2001*, for example – but only occasionally in the mainstream. The fluid T-1000 of *Terminator 2* has the protean potential to take on any shape, but tends to adopt the form of familiar objects and individuals. Designs that attempt to capture a sense of otherness are often rapidly adopted as part of the vocabulary of science fiction cinema and therefore rendered familiar. 'We thought this would make things easier for you', says the alien presence visited in *Contact*, appearing in the guise of the protagonist's father on a reproduction of a Florida beach; familiar images avoid too great a shock for the character, Ellie Arroway. A cynic might add that they can also save the film-makers considerable expense and any leap of the design imagination. A combination of both strange and familiar visions is found in *Solaris*: an alien presence haunts the occupants of a Soviet space station in recognisable shapes drawn from their memories, yet the entity itself is figured in the inchoate form of an oceanic planetary intelligence.

Interactivity and Immersion: Beyond the Second Dimension

Science fiction cinema promises to transport us to new worlds. It should not be surprising, then, that science fiction is so prominent in new media forms such as virtual reality simulation and computer games that explore dimensions of *immersion** and *interactivity**: new ways of actually taking us *into* the fictional universe. A distinct sub-genre of science fiction cinema has begun to explore these dimensions at a thematic level. But science fiction has also become a favourite choice for products beginning to make direct use of interactive or immersive technologies.

The facility to interact with narratives to some extent has become a significant marketing device, especially as many film producers and distributors have a large stake in the development of computer-based media. Computer games, virtual reality and DVD offer a marketable difference from the medium of film, giving the user the ability to interact with a text. Computer and video games offer a good deal of freedom, allowing the player to control the journey of the main character through the game. Many of these are based on science fiction films, including an ever-growing number of *Star Wars* and *Star Trek* products. Many new science fiction blockbusters find their way onto the games shelf in one shape or another, making the form an important source of revenue for the film industry. Several other games, including the blockbuster hits *Doom* (GT/id software) and *Tomb Raider* (Core/Eidos), draw at least partly on science fiction sources.

Games are often marketed as distinct from the passive experience of watching a film, but they nevertheless rely on familiar film devices such as the use of special effects, continuity editing, narrative coherence and the presence of a central hero or heroine. Players are given space to interact with, and to some extent inhabit, the three-dimensional world of the game. Games offer the opportunity to enter into the world of a favourite movie, to repeat the actions of its heroes or to linger and explore areas passed over too rapidly on screen. They can also offer new combinations of science fiction adventures. The recent *Alien vs. Predator* (Fox Interactive), for example, enables players to match the respective abilities of two formidable alien foes. Gameboy's *Pokémon* (Nintendo) is based on a Japanese TV Manga series designed for children. It draws on Manga's cute animation style, but goes further in allowing children to collect the computerised Pokémon creatures and play 'swaps' with their friends: 'gotta catch 'em all', as the theme tune suggests to promote greater spending.

Virtual reality is based on the promise of freeing the user from the two-dimensionality of the flat screen. The aim is to immerse the user in a synthetic three-dimensional experience, a world that can be inhabited physically by connecting the head and body to an array of visual, touch and motion sensors. Full-scale virtual reality of any great resolution remains something of a developer's dream, certainly as a medium for any kind of substantial representation and protracted engagement. A limited version of immersion – if not interactivity – is offered by a new generation of theme park attractions, many of which are based on science fiction films. Motion simulator platforms based on those developed by the US military are used in attractions such as Disneyland's *Star Tours* and *Back to the Future: The Ride*, at Universal Studios, to create an illusion of participation in scenes taken or extrapolated from the films. Universal's *Terminator 2: 3D* offers a miniature sequel to the two cinematic versions, in which 3D imagery is combined with live-action performance and physical effects such as shifting seats, smoke and liquid sprays to create some degree of illusion of sharing the virtual space of the fictional characters. A similar approach is taken by Disneyland's *Honey, I Shrunk the Audience*.

A more encompassing form of virtual reality, or some kind of immersion in the world of the computer game, remains a subject of great speculation and appeal. Fictional contemplations about the possible futures of immersive virtual reality and interactivity are present in many recent science fiction films, from *Tron* to *The Matrix*. Their extrapolations from existing virtual technologies offer ways of exploring many of the issues discussed in Section 1 of this book, while the depiction of virtual reality dreamscapes offers scope for the obligatory quota of vivid special effects. *The Lawnmower Man* and *Strange Days* provide useful examples of the way Hollywood science fiction has embraced the idea of virtual reality and advanced computer games. The virtual world of *The Lawnmower Man*, and that of many later virtual reality films, represents the excitement of interactive games, the possibility of freedom from the limitations of the body (see Sobchack 1993), but also fears of what might result: in this case the global dominance of one virtual megalomaniac. The fictional SQUID technology in *Strange Days* allows people to record their emotional and physical experiences. The user is able to inhabit these second-hand experiences – with all their transgressive, visceral and emotional sensations – but with the advantage of being able to switch off the technology. *Strange Days* likens this to the black-market world of drugs and worries about the dangers of its habit-forming use. The SQUID

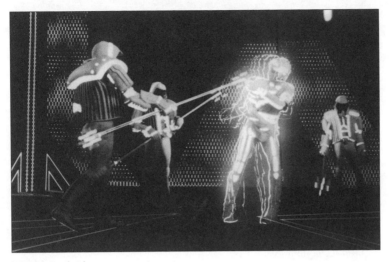

FIGURE 9 *Tron (1982)*

playback system is not interactive but immersive and passive, more like film itself. The depiction of the 'clips', however, mirrors the familiar use of point-of-view shots in contemporary computer games. As such it connotes the pleasures and cultural currency of interactivity without going beyond a heightened form of immersion.

The spectacular new landscapes offered by the digital world that have captured the contemporary science fiction imagination are very different from the low-tech effects of the aliens-from-space 1950s B-movie. In these films outer space has been replaced by digital 'inner' space as the new frontier. In accordance with the dystopian world of cyberpunk novels, digital space is often figured as a form of labyrinthine Dante's inferno, inhabited by the souls or ghosts of people who have 'uploaded' themselves on the death of their material body, as in *Johnny Mnemonic*, the screenplay for which was written by William Gibson, and *Spawn* (1997). It may be figured as a busy information highway, which can be accessed for subversive purposes, or it might be an embryonic utopia (although this is often a seductive promise that turns 'bad'). All of these possibilities are combined in films such as *The Lawnmower Man*, *Johnny*

Mnemonic, *Strange Days* and *The Matrix*, playing perhaps on a range of contemporary hopes and anxieties about morality, humanity and mortality in the extended world of the digital age.

The aim of making films fully interactive, rather than just taking the subject as a narrative theme, is now being realised to a limited extent in DVD technology. Like computer games and CD-ROM, DVD offers the possibility of films that have multiple routes through the story, a shift from the closed narratives of previous science fiction films (for more on interactive narratives see Murray 1997; Landow 1992). More developed interactive forms might alter our conception of film, giving us more control over the sequence of events. This could make film watching – or film 'playing' – a more isolated, domestic and individual experience, unlike the communal event provided by the drive-in or multiplex, although it is as yet unclear exactly what directions might be taken or how much demand exists for interactive narrative.

Interactive formats might undermine some of our familiar narrative pleasures. Much of the impact of cinematic and other narrative is based on the fact that we do not control the supply of information or know exactly which directions a story will take. To give too much control to the viewer/user might rob the experience of its dramatic and emotional tension. Many media companies are investing heavily in the development of interactive computer technologies, however, following a precedent set by George Lucas, whose LucasArts Entertainment division develops computer games. The proponents of immersive and interactive media suggest that it is no longer enough to sit back and watch the spectacle, in science fiction especially. We are offered, instead, the prospect of joining in, triggering the outbursts of special effects ourselves, in the guise of our on-screen avatars. The cinema of science fiction, perhaps more than any other genre, is wrestling with the very parameters of the medium. It remains open to question how much is really likely to change. The themes explored by interactive or immersive forms of science fiction are generally familiar ones from the genre and there is no evidence of any near-future shift to a radically new dimension of big-screen entertainment – an extrapolation that remains primarily the stuff of science fiction itself.

3   CASE STUDY: *STAR WARS: EPISODE I –*
     THE PHANTOM MENACE

Love it or loathe it, but you cannot easily ignore it. When a new episode of
the Star Wars cycle comes out it forces itself on our consciousness. From
burger wrappers to computer games, from TV adverts to the covers of
magazines as diverse as *Vogue* and *Popular Mechanics*, the carpet-
bombing promotion strategy used for *Star Wars: Episode I – The Phantom
Menace* is a defining aspect of the successful event movie. The marketing
strategy seeks to create an irresistible momentum, exploiting every
conceivable aspect of merchandising and mass media, a process honed
to a fine if not always subtle art by those involved in the selling of *The
Phantom Menace*. The aim is to rekindle the enthusiasm of older viewers
for the *Star Wars* cycle and to recruit new viewers among younger people
and children. The perfect event movie, and any *Star Wars* film is an ideal
candidate, becomes something we feel almost *obliged* to see, and on
which we are required to have an opinion if we are to participate fully in
the popular culture of our time.

   The Phantom Menace cost a hefty $115 million to make but a great deal
more was probably spent on promotion, an imbalance that has become an
obligatory feature of the contemporary blockbuster. The average Hollywood budget in 1999 was put at $51.4 million. The average marketing cost
was $24.53 million (figures from the Motion Picture Association of
America, *1999 US Economic Review*). These are overall averages, however:
the proportion spent on marketing tends to be higher on blockbusters,

hugely so if we include the sums invested by outside companies buying the rights to use blockbuster brand names on their products. To give one example, although only marginally within the genre of science fiction, the James Bond film *GoldenEye* (1995), made on a budget of $50 million, is reported to have received as much again in promotional tie-in payments from companies including BMW, Omega watches, and Yves Saint Laurent (Lukk 1997: 59). Such was the market value of *The Phantom Menace* that very little of the promotional budget had to be picked up by the production company, Lucasfilm, or the distributor Twentieth Century Fox; almost all of these costs were met by companies licensed to use the film's name in their own marketing or spin-off production (see Kaplan 1999). As far as the producers and distributors were concerned, the film had the status largely to market itself. The only real issue was how to handle the process, to build anticipation to precisely the right crescendo, peaking neither too early nor to late to gain the maximum return.

The release of a film as keenly anticipated as *The Phantom Menace* sheds light on some of the key power relationships within the business. The exhibition sector makes plenty of profit from such films, of course, but is in a relatively weak position in relation to distributors and/or production companies. To gain access to a film vital to their trade in 1999, cinema chains had to fulfil a range of conditions: one example being that the film had to be guaranteed minimum runs of at least two or three months in the biggest screens of the most prestigious theatres (see, again, Kaplan 1999).

Distribution is usually the key site of power in contemporary Hollywood. The big-name major studios are now principally financiers and distributors of films, actually producing relatively few titles themselves. *The Phantom Menace* is unusual in this respect. It was financed by Lucasfilm, the company owned by George Lucas, which retained control over the division of the financial spoils. How much the film will eventually earn remains to be seen. At the time of writing it had grossed nearly $800 million worldwide and reached the number three slot in the all-time box-office league (on the basis of figures not adjusted for inflation; the use of these statistics is encouraged by the industry as it has a built-in tendency to magnify the status of the latest features).

Merchandising and other spin-off products are not just designed to get more people into the cinema. A film like *The Phantom Menace* is likely to earn far greater revenues through the sale of books, games, toys and just about every kind of product imaginable. One estimate put the expected figure at about £2.5 billion (Cole 2000: 25). Hordes of manufacturers were licensed to produce items based on the film, while burger chains and soft-drinks companies competed for the right to use *The Phantom Menace* images in their advertising or packaging. George Lucas insisted on retaining the merchandising rights to the original *Star Wars* films, a canny move at a time when merchandising was not established as a major source of profit, and continues to earn huge sums from products bearing the brand. Connections with blockbuster films, however arbitrary, are attractive marketing hooks for producers of all sorts of goods. But they are not infallible. Some toy manufacturers steer clear of film tie-ins, which are considered unpredictable (Wasko 1994: 207). Even so keenly anticipated an attraction as *The Phantom Menace* lost its halo for some participants, notably the publisher Dorling Kindersley, which sold only three million of 13 million tie-in books, losing a hefty £18 million in the process (Cole 2000: 24). Expectations were excessive, tempting the company to over-invest in what might have appeared to be a sure-fire winner. Dorling Kindersley was not alone. The American toy giant Hasbro also suffered lower sales than anticipated (25). The fast food chain that owns Kentucky Fried Chicken, Taco Bell and Pizza Hut in the United States was reported to have been disappointed by the effect of its *Phantom Menace* promotion on sales (*Sight and Sound*, September 1999: 5). Toy manufacturers also complained about the pre-release secrecy imposed on *Godzilla*, which was thought to have reduced the level of sales of the huge volumes of merchandise produced to accompany the film.

If a blockbuster film is to recoup its large financial investment and turn in heavy profits it must reach a huge audience, beyond America and beyond the confines of the core groups that go to the movies on a regular basis. This necessity is an important factor in shaping the way the story is structured. The blockbuster usually needs to address a broad range of ages, genders and cultural backgrounds. *The Phantom Menace* thus provides several different types of characters as possible sources of audience identification. The young and 'gifted' Anakin Skywalker (Jake Lloyd) is designed to appeal to boys of a similar age, offering a seductive fantasy of technological mastery and escape from domestic banalities. The pair of Jedi knights, with their special powers and licence to kill, might appeal, respectively, to teenagers and adults. The older and wiser Qui-Gon Jinn (Liam Neeson) offers a more mature perspective, perhaps, for all those parents dragged to see the film by their children. The casting of Ewan McGregor in the role of Obi-Wan Kenobi provides a link to contemporary youth culture. Jar Jar Binks, the bungling computer-generated Gungan, offers a more obvious point of identification for younger children. A less heroic figure, he provides much of the film's humour. His blunders have a way of turning out for the good, however, which perhaps speaks to children, whose lives revolve around the trials and errors of the learning process. Audience reaction in screenings suggests that the antics of Jar Jar are a major source of pleasure for children, which might account for his heavy presence in the film's merchandise.

The extent to which this range of characters is explicitly designed to reach the sections of the audience suggested here remains a subject for further investigation. Hollywood tends to remain secretive about such strategic planning, preferring to foster the illusion that its products spring fully formed either from the imagination of their authors or from popular demand, rather than being the outcome of protracted market analysis and pre-testing (for a detailed account of this process in relation to *Star Wars*, see Earnest 1985). The imperative to offer a range of audience appeals, especially within particular combinations of segments, is a powerful one, however, and likely to be a major factor in the design of blockbuster products and merchandising.

Anakin, the Jedi knights and Jar Jar provide a variety of different characters with which the audience can identify. The lack of much in the way of appealing female characters suggests that the film is targeted initially at an audience of boys and men. Queen Amidala (Natalie Portman) is a central character, but rather dull and uninvolving. There is also Anakin's mother, but her role is restricted to a stereotypical act of maternal sacrifice, while Queen Amidala's handmaidens play little active part. Most tellingly, perhaps, the female characters are denied much interaction with trade-mark technologies such as lightsabers and pod-racers, the carriers of greatest prestige. The earlier films had their limitations in terms of character and relationships, but did at least reserve a central place for the romantic interest between Princess Leia (Carrie Fisher), Luke Skywalker (Mark Hammil) and Han Solo (Harrison Ford). Leia's feisty nature and the initial competition set up for her affections between Han and Luke was important to the film's potential address to a female audience.

The fact that initial title and concept tests indicated that *Star Wars* was likely to appeal largely to young males influenced the shape of the advertising campaign eventually used for the film: a greater emphasis was placed on 'fantasy' and the human element, rather than just on what was seen as male-oriented 'science fiction' (Earnest 1985). It is curious that *The Phantom Menace* assigns such a marginal role to women and does not develop a central romance plot, especially given the box-office lesson provided by *Titanic* (1997), much of the success of which has been credited to multiple viewing by young women (see Kramer 1998). In comparison with the wooden Queen Amidala, Princess Leia has the dynamism that characterises more recent tough but tender roles (Buffy or Xena on television, for instance). That is not to say that the lack of such a female character will necessarily be a bar to pleasure for women and girls in the audience. The predominant appeal to a male audience is further embedded at a subtextual level, discussed below, as well as in the 'toys for the boys' element that underlies most of the film's set-piece special effects sequences.

The pod-race sequence, a high-speed blur of action in which the young Anakin Skywalker competes against a motley array of other beings, offers a useful way to explore a number of issues to do with the film's status as special effects-based spectacle, another key feature of the contemporary science fiction blockbuster. One of the most striking features of the sequence is its resemblance to a computer game. It is hardly surprising to find that there is a game based on the race, *Star Wars: Episode 1 – Racer* (LucasArts), which, initially at least, outsold the game based on the entire film. The pod-race offers a combination of views of the action. First-person shots, in which we appear to take on the perspective of Anakin, are intercut with a range of other viewpoints: apparently neutral 'objective' shots and those approximate to the perspectives of spectators, including the other principal characters. Similar perspectives are offered when this kind of race or pursuit action is provided by computer games, which commonly offer the player a choice of first or third person vantage points. *Racer* provides four angles on the action. The kinds of movements that are involved – high speed ducking and weaving around the alarming contours of the racetrack – are the familiar stuff of computer games, and of film-based rides. It remains to be seen whether the sequence eventually becomes translated into a ride alongside *Star Tours* at Disneyland, a format to which it would be ideally suited.

To what extent does a film like *The Phantom Menace* exist primarily to act as an engine for the generation of profitable spin-offs such as the *Racer* game? Is a sequence like the pod-race included in order to be translated into a computer game, or is this just a 'value-added' benefit? How central are such factors to the calculations of those who design these big-screen products? Which comes first: the race as an integral part of the film, or the intention to extract it for other purposes? Questions like this are difficult to answer definitively, as this is a subject film-makers or production executives are unlikely to discuss in public. It does not much matter, anyway. More significant is what the existence of such spin-offs tells us about the broader industrial context: a world of entertainment conglomerates built around the multiple exploitation of profitable franchises such as the *Star Wars* series brand. The relationship between the pod-race and the rest of the film is also part of a more general issue about the implications of special effects extravaganzas in contemporary Hollywood science fiction.

How exactly does the pod-race sequence fit into the overall structure of *The Phantom Menace*? A common complaint in recent criticism, both academic and more general, is that impressive effects sequences have little relation to plot, story or character; that they are loosely strung together with little concern for narrative. It is easy to see how this accusation could be made of the pod-race and other spectacular aspects of *The Phantom Menace*. The race is quite protracted: it lasts some seven minutes, an unusually extended period over which to sustain such blistering-paced action. This sequence – and many others in the film – is clearly designed to provide the kind of spectacle that has become so important in Hollywood cinema, particularly science fiction.

It is easy to overstate the case for this kind of film as purely an exercise in jaw-dropping spectacle. The pod-race also serves narrative purposes, some more nuanced than others. The whole business of the race is thoroughly motivated in terms of the basic forward movement of the plot. Qui-Gon Jinn arranges a series of wagers on the race, the terms of which mean a victory for Anakin will allow the principal characters to get their spaceship fixed and continue their journey. And with their journey, of course, goes the main plot of the film: if the two Jedi and the rest of their party are stuck on Tatooine, the narrative has nowhere much to go. Anakin is also racing to secure his own freedom from slavery, although he is not aware of this at the time, an issue that is also of broader relevance to the long narrative arc transcribed not just by *The Phantom Menace* but the entire *Star Wars* series. There is much at stake. This said, it could still be argued that, once it has started, the race sequence offers a kind of entertainment that is firmly bracketed off from these narrative concerns. It is to some extent, although the race has its own miniature narrative structure as well, a pattern that can be seen as a microcosm of the typical shape of Hollywood fiction: a beginning, middle and end organised around a series of problems to be overcome by the protagonist.

There is probably not a great deal of tension or suspense involved in the resolution of the plot elements tied up with the race. Viewers are unlikely to have much doubt about the probable outcome, given the familiar conventions of this kind of science fiction fantasy, and the fact that we *know* the plot is unlikely to come to a standstill, marooned on the desert planet, an hour into the film. The race is given a carefully honed structure, however, in an effort to construct an element of suspense, increased by the belated revelation that Anakin has to date never actually finished a race. The race starts with Anakin's racer sabotaged and stalled on the grid. He loses a great deal of ground and eventually catches up. He is hit by sabotage again before finally making up the ground once more and zipping to a last-minute victory. This is standard Hollywood stuff, the outsider who comes back against adversity, more than once, to earn an unlikely fanfare of triumph – the material of any number of *Rocky*-type parables. No great claims could be made for this miniature narrative, but it is a narrative nonetheless, and one that is worked into the heart of a significant slice of the spectacle offered by *The Phantom Menace*. It is helpful to avoid any confusion between judgements about the *quality* of narrative elements such as this, which may not be terribly high, and the question of whether narrative is significantly present at all.

Two rather different questions are involved. A film like *The Phantom Menace* is unlikely to win any prizes or critical plaudits for the complexity or subtlety of its narrative. But it does have plenty of narrative, and at more than one level. On the largest scale, the film has to be seen in the context of the serial structure of the entire six- or nine-film *Star Wars* project envisioned by George Lucas. Unlike space serials shown at closely-spaced intervals, such as on television or in the 1930s and 1940s serial format of *Flash Gordon* and *Buck Rogers*, the films do not appear on a weekly or seasonal basis, which complicates their narrative structure. The four episodes to date have been spread over a period of twenty-two years and, with the move back to 'Episode I', are no longer delivered in linear order. This has implications for the shape of each episode and its ability to maintain a clear sense of cohesion. This is achieved, partly, through the central presence of the relationship between Luke Skywalker and his father, Darth Vader. Their relationship crystallises a battle between the forces of good and evil that invokes a whole gamut of mythic resonances.

This initially rather simplistic mapping aids the process of orientation across the length of the narrative. Extratextual dimensions such as merchandising and multimedia exploitation enhance narrative coherence and ongoing interest in the basic situation of plot and characters.

Even more diffusely, the series also gains from the extent to which the scenario and characters have penetrated western culture: *Star Wars* terminology abounds in many places, from sit-com to the arms race. This has helped George Lucas to continue to produce episodes over a long period of time, each episode telling its own story, but these stories slot into a broadly familiar overall scheme. Narrative enigmas are planted to create gaps in the knowledge of the viewer, designed to create hunger for the next episode. Will Anakin Skywalker turn out to be good or evil? *The Phantom Menace* leaves this question open and the audience perspective on such issues depends on how well they know the previous episodes. Anyone who remembers *Return of the Jedi* (1983), the third part of the initial trilogy, may recall that Anakin was the name of Darth Vader before he crossed over to the 'dark side', and will therefore know the answer to that particular enigma. Plenty of other intertextual sources, including publicity material for *The Phantom Menace*, are available to confirm this kind of background data. But other questions remain. How exactly does Anakin become the evil Vader, for example, and what is the full story of his parentage? These are blatant gaps left in the narrative of *The Phantom Menace*, gaps that we can expect to be filled if we maintain our commitment to the ongoing adventure. Like a soap opera or a television serial, a science fiction saga of this kind tries to include detail and to draw on existing background knowledge that rewards the devotee without leaving the more casual viewer alienated or confused.

However spectacular, *The Phantom Menace* retains a strong commitment to the narrative dimension, although it might not entirely succeed in making the larger structure clear to the uninitiated. We can return here to nuances in the computer game-like characteristics of the pod-race that have implications for narrative issues. On closer inspection there are actually relatively few subjective shots of the race from Anakin's point-of-view, certainly fewer than are likely to be used by a player of the game.

There might be a perfectly simple formal explanation for this, including the excessively dizzying impact on the big-screen viewer that might have resulted. But we could probe further. We might consider what is implied by a first-person perspective. It usually suggests that some kind of identification is being encouraged between character and viewer. Anakin, however, even at this relatively early stage, remains an ambiguous figure. A potent source of connection with the 'Force', but also, as Yoda indicates, potentially dangerous and maybe a figure from whom we should maintain safe distance. Younger viewers are likely to identify with Anakin more wholeheartedly, especially during sequences such as the pod-race, where doubts about his future status remain in the background. They might be entirely oblivious to the fact that he is destined to become Darth Vader; they might know, but forget, or not bring that knowledge to bear on the experience of the pod-race spectacle.

Like most films, *The Phantom Menace* is open to a variety of levels of reading, a dimension especially relevant to blockbusters designed to appeal to a broad audience, ranging from knowing adult fans to young children. For some, the broader narrative frame will be a constant reference point for smaller details. Others might watch the film in a more compartmentalised manner, enjoying the dynamics of what is immediately on offer in one sequence or another. A more diffuse combination of both approaches might be experienced by many viewers, although none of these strategies are easy (if possible) to quantify. It might be that the pod-race sequence would have been shot in exactly the same manner if no doubts were to be cast about Anakin's ultimate place in the equation between good and evil. First-person perspectives are usually used sparingly in such sequences. Should we read more into this? Formal qualities can usefully be explored in this way for thematic implications, but there is no ultimate point of proof or evidence to which we can appeal to settle such issues (indeed many films trade on such ambiguities which may help promote post-film discussion and 'fan' culture).

We can go further, however, to examine the pod-race sequence, and other spectacular sequences, in terms of the underlying thematic issues discussed in Section 1. *The Phantom Menace* engages in the broad question of the relationship between the realms of technology and humanity explored in so much science fiction. The Trade Federation, which illegally invades the planet of Naboo, is presented as the forerunner of the evil Empire of the later *Star Wars* films. The Empire, in its later incarnations, has at its heart a combination of the rational and the mystical, a technologically-based military might aided by the less material powers of the dark side of the Force in the shape of the Emperor and Darth Vader. The series plays around discourses that might offer some reconciliation of troubling cultural oppositions between these two realms. The shadowy figure who will later emerge as the power behind the Empire lurks under the façade of the Trade Federation in *The Phantom Menace*, although the Federation itself appears to put its trust firmly in the direction of technology. Much of the work of invading Naboo is put in the hands of mechanical droids controlled from an orbiting spaceship.

Anakin, as possessor of a strong affinity with the Force, is aligned with the opposition to the Trade Federation's technological might, a characteristic that is present if not fully developed in the pod-race. Qui-Gon Jinn advises Anakin to rely on his feelings rather than (rational) thoughts, and it appears to be non-rational power that ensures his victory. The race is thus made to echo the climactic assault on the Death Star in the original *Star Wars* (subsequently styled as *Episode IV – A New Hope*) in which the mature Obi-Wan Kenobi advises Luke Skywalker to use the Force rather than his technological guidance system. Technological might, in both episodes, is revealed as vulnerable to more instinctive and intuitive interventions. It is no accident that it is Anakin, seemingly unintentionally, who brings about the defeat of the massive droid army by the Gungan resistance on Naboo.

Haplessly joining an attempted aerial assault on the Trade Federation battleship – he is supposed to be hiding in the cockpit and takes off on the mission only after fumbling randomly at the controls – Anakin manages, again without intention, to land his fighter on the enemy vessel. Opening fire haphazardly on the force that greets his landing, he succeeds quite by chance in destroying the ship's central power unit, thus disabling the myriad droids on the planet surface and saving the day. Quirky 'human'-style intervention thus triumphs over technological regimenta-tion, a characteristic we have identified elsewhere in contemporary science fiction cinema. *The Phantom Menace* however, like the other films in the series, goes a stage further. In the notion of the Force, the series formalises the otherwise amorphous conception of whatever it is that stands in opposition to dependence on the rational-technological. This is a significant moment, one in which qualities that are usually unstated and implicit are brought to the surface and given both a name and a mystical dimension. Nothing happens by accident, Qui-Gon declares of his meeting with Anakin on Tatooine, thus seeming to square the circle, rhetorically at least, between the options of rational-technological determinism and all-out coincidence. The Force enables special effects magic to be linked with the fantasy worlds of myth and mystery. It is here that the *Star Wars* cycle leans upon older narratives such as that of Arthur, Merlin and the Knights of the Round Table. Each is framed by a struggle between good and evil. Such parallels lend the science fiction saga the quality of dynastic epic familiar in mythology.

If the *seemingly* accidental appears to characterise Anakin's destruc-tion of the droid control ship, something of the same dynamic seems to characterise the battle on the ground. A vast army of droids, destroyer-droids and formidable battle tanks are deployed against an inferior force of Gungans, led partly by the unlikely figure of Jar Jar Binks. By any rational standards, the Gungans, with their more primitive 'energy ball' weapons, are in for a beating. But, even before Anakin's success, there are signs of gain through sheer haphazardry. Jar Jar himself, banished from Gunga for his susceptibility to mishap, manages to despatch a number of droids purely by accident during his cowardly-farcical antics. On the broader canvas, the battles present us with a juxtaposition at the design level between the sleek and massively reproduced technology of droid war-culture (losers) and the clumsily organic and animal-like Gungans (styled as highly unlikely victors).

An interesting manoeuvre seems to be involved here, shifting us from the register of diegetic narrative themes to those that leak over into considerations of the nature of the film itself as technological artefact. Both battlefield opponents owe their textual existence to state-of-the-art special effects technologies; both are entirely artificial creations. One, however, is cast as essentially organic and quirky. In fact, the principal Gungan, Jar Jar Binks, is by far the most 'human'-seeming figure in the film, given the one-dimensional portrayal of the Jedi principals and Queen Amidala. In other words a form of film-making heavily reliant on technology is subjected to the kind of separation that is often characteristic of ideological manoeuvres. One portion is condemned, righteously, for its cold rationality, while another is 'saved' by being pulled across the line around which key textual oppositions revolve: in this case, the computer-generated Gungans, rendered with many of the qualities associated with a particular version of 'humanity' – quirky, comic and emotional. This may be important in terms of the debates surrounding a film like *The Phantom Menace*, in which accusations of over-reliance on the technological domain of special effects enter a public arena much broader than the confines of academic debate.

Like the other films in the series, *The Phantom Menace* bases much of its spectacular visual appeal on the display of a multitude of strikingly different imaginary locales. It offers a kind of galactic travelogue, a science fiction equivalent of the assorted 'exotic' locations that have become an obligatory ingredient of the James Bond series. This is important in itself, as sheer spectacle, but can in some cases be linked to thematic concerns. Organic qualities dominate the globular underwater city of the Gungans, one of the most imaginative and impressive fantasy worlds presented by the film. The circularity of its chambers is replicated in the energy ball weapons and the domed shield generated over the Gungan warriors during the battle with the droids. The underwater city shimmers with a 'natural' greenish tone. Similar characteristics are suggested by the tangled and misty swamps of Naboo and, in harsher vein, the desert world of Tatooine. The location that seems most representative of the Trade Federation's reliance on technology is the battleship from which the invasion of Naboo is led, a giant and supposedly invulnerable curved structure built around a central sphere.

Its shape suggests something of Saturn and its rings, a reminder of the deadly artificial planet Death Star in the original trilogy.

The film also displays spectacular locations that are more equivocal in their associations. The galactic capital Coruscant is a planet-wide cityscape that offers classic futuristic science fiction vistas of prodigious edifices and skies teeming with flying traffic. Here we find the galactic senate, a body that meets in a huge circular chamber, the delegates occupying floating pods that move to the fore when they are called to speak. This might be an image of democratic openness on a large scale, but the enormity of the structure and the undertones of delay and plotting accompanying the sequences in the chamber suggest a source of bureaucratic inertia, a Kafkaesque quality in the vertiginous space within which it is hard to maintain any bearings. Coruscant could easily be a site of metropolitan evil, juxtaposed to the more 'natural' environments of *The Phantom Menace*; but it is also the home of a Jedi temple, a font of goodness, although also in its way a formal institution marked in opposition to the instincts of the Jedi hero Qui-Gon Jinn.

Another location that seems to carry a mixture of potentials in its designs is the city of Theed on Naboo. The palace and gardens of Queen Amidala stand in contrast to the swamp and underwater world of the neighbouring Gungans. One is formal, marked in geometrical patterns and structures; the other more chaotic and abundant. The Naboo, and Amidala in particular, are presented as somewhat aloof and superior in manner, a fact resented by the rotund Gungan leader, Boss Nass. The Naboo are largely sympathetic figures, the innocent victims of imperialist occupation, but are also forced into an accommodation with the Gungans to prevent being overrun. A rather 'over-civilised' culture is thus reconciled with one from the 'lower' depths closer to nature: the result, presumably, will be an ideal combination. Most of what we see of the city has a 'classical' quality, suggestive of royal palaces and gardens closer to home. It also includes more characteristically hi-tech science fiction realms, such as the power-generating complex. This is a location typical of the *Star Wars* tradition, decked out in neon and marbled surfaces, with platforms and ledges suitable for lightsaber duels between the Jedi and

Darth Maul and vast abyssal chasms reminiscent of the massive scale of the Krel technology in *Forbidden Planet*. Another mixture of the technological and a more recent version of the classical is found in Amidala's royal starship, a gloriously streamlined silver construction that might be more at home in a film of the 1950s than amid the often darker and more functional craft of 1990s science fiction.

The costume and make-up designs of *The Phantom Menace* favour a mixture of the gothic and the oriental over anything very futuristic. The gothic is most strongly apparent in Darth Maul's demonic horns and the red and black make-up mask that borrows from the facial designs found in depictions of Japanese demons. Maul and Darth Sidious are cloaked in black robes. Qui-Gon and Obi-Wan also wear tunics and hooded robes, but these have a softer brown hue than those of their enemies. The Jedi outfits are the ritual garb of a religious warrior order. Their lightsabers combine the qualities of ancient and futuristic, the sword and the hi-tech buzz. Qui-Gon's pony tail and Obi-Wan's position as apprentice further encourage a reading in terms of the Samurai tradition. Amidala, in keeping with her status and character, has a number of highly formal outfits (merchandised, naturally, to fit the Amidala doll) to go with hair sculpted into a curve that frames make-up of a Japanese cast. The character of Amidala is overwhelmed by costume: she is a figurehead dressed to mark her off from the masses. She seems only able to speak for herself when dressed in the plainer clothes of the handmaiden, an identity she assumes during the visit to Tatooine. Only then does her expressionless tone give way to something more impassioned and her movements become less constrained.

On Tatooine, the prevailing look is one of straitened practicality, a design aesthetic closer to the post-apocalyptic with its rough, homespun clothing and technologies such as pod-racers constructed from scavenged remains. The film offers an eclectic mix of designs that serve various purposes. Plurality of design creates visual interest and can also be interpreted in terms of the thematic issues raised by the film. We should not forget the importance of merchandising, however, as a major factor in the design of *The Phantom Menace*. The different costume designs have thematic and narrative relevance, but perhaps serve a more immediate purpose in providing a range of clearly identifiable characters to be sold as figurines or to decorate other spin-off products.

Costume and special make-up designs also figure centrally in the construction of the diverse groups of aliens and humans of different races and cultures that make up the Federation and the Jedi council displayed in *The Phantom Menace*. On the surface it would appear that the film, like *Star Trek* and the television series *Babylon 5* (1994–1995), is touting a liberal multi-cultural message, although the multitude of characters is also driven to some extent by its potential for further merchandising. Unlike the alien invaders of the 1950s B-movie or the radically othered monsters of the *Alien* quartet, the alien races in *The Phantom Menace* are rarely presented as inherently evil. Humans and aliens alike may choose to be corrupt or serve the dark side. This seems enlightened enough, but is undermined by a great deal of crude cultural stereotyping. The Gungans are presented generally as a cowardly and lackadaisical group. This might be acceptable as a fictional characterisation if not for the fact that they are given clearly Afro-Caribbean traits. Jar Jar Binks, the amiable but rather stupid and naïve comic fop, is voiced by a black American actor in a classic transcription of the racist caricature of the 'Coon', a stereotype that has served for many decades to excuse or justify racial inequality (see Bogle 1993). On Tatooine, the grasping spare parts entrepreneur Watto is grossly caricatured as a hook-nosed bug, an apparent case of anti-semitism. The Neimoidian trade viceroys who betray the inhabitants of Naboo to the Sith, meanwhile, are given Japanese-style costumes and accents. While the federation of inter-galactic nations ostensibly speaks out against the tyranny of Nazi-like regimentation, the film risks alienating potential audience groups often for the sake of a cheap laugh.

Delving deeper into the implications of the narrative for its gender politics, it becomes clear that a dominant notion of masculinity is sustained by the film. The principal heroes are white males (Qui-Gon Jinn, Obi-Wan Kenobi and Anakin Skywalker), figures with access to the Force. How, exactly, is this 'Force' described? Previous episodes established it as some kind of invisible cosmic power. *The Phantom Menace* introduces a new element of explanation, including a biological dimension. Communication with the Force is achieved through microscopic life-forms called 'midi-chlorians', which reside in all living cells but are found in higher concentrations in the potential Jedi knight. Anakin, Qui-Gon discovers, has an exceptionally high midi-chlorian level. The Force itself is extraneous to the individual, but can be mobilised with the correct discipline and training. The Force is out of balance, we are told, and the Jedi are looking for a figure who will restore its balance. We may recall from 'earlier' episodes that this will prove to be Luke not Anakin, despite Qui-Gon's faith in the latter. It is, however, possible to interpret the Force as having a demonic element. As communication with the Force is determined by life-forms that reside in the body, it is equivalent in some ways to the invasive forces that appear in the horror film and science fiction/horror hybrids. In the possession film, the act of being possessed is usually gendered feminine (see Clover 1992). The possessing agent penetrates the body and wrests control from the victim, which is anathema to the individual autonomy that defines Western conceptions of masculinity (and of humanity in general, the two often being conflated). The film is very careful to constrain its definition of the Force, therefore, in order not to feminise its heroes (the fact that Leia is Luke's brother – Vader's daughter – and also has access to the Force is left largely undeveloped at the end of the initial trilogy). But here lies an interesting ambiguity. The Jedi knight is said to 'use' the Force by letting it guide his actions. This suggests that he is no longer in control, allowing the Force to work through him. At the same time there is a constant stress on the idea of control and discipline, which works to hold in abeyance the potential feminisation implied by possession. *Star Wars* hedges its bets, suggesting that the Force both controls the actions and obeys the commands of the adept.

The Star Wars cycle appears to be a fairly simple and familiar story of struggle between the forces of good and evil. Beneath this and the gloss of spectacular effects is a very masculine bias. It is men who hold the key to the destiny of the universe; it hinges around relationships between father and son, master and apprentice. This boils down to a contest for power and control reflected in the theme of mastery that circulates around the use of technology and the 'correct' application of the Force. In *The Phantom Menace*, Anakin seems to have found a good father figure in Obi-Wan Kenobi, as did Luke in the older Obi-Wan and Yoda. As it stands at the end of the film, Anakin has been apprenticed to Obi-Wan Kenobi, against Yoda's advice. As Darth Maul is now dead (cut in half by Obi-Wan), his master is looking for a new apprentice to enter into a pact with the dark side, taking the saga into a new cycle in the next episode.

The enormous success of the *Star Wars* series, including *The Phantom Menace*, suggests the films are engaged at some level in an exploration of issues that have currency in the broader cultural context. Lucas brings together a story derived from a blend of traditional myths and popular culture. This strategy of linking the archaic and the contemporary aims to evoke mythic narratives seen as defining humanity more generally. Lucas has made reference in interviews to the influence of Joseph Campbell's studies of the function of mythology. In *The Hero with a Thousand Faces* (1949), Campbell often focuses on the male initiatory journey dominant in many myths, and it is these that figure most strongly in the *Star Wars* cycle. The use of this kind of mythical content, and the reliance on Campbell's view that myths speak of universal truths about the nature of humanity, is ideologically loaded. Appeals to universality tend to obscure the effects of culture and history. Values and investments specific to a certain race, class or gendered group are treated as if they were somehow timeless and inevitable. We should remember that the heroic figures of *The Phantom Menace* are white males, constructed according to the dictates of a white and male-dominated society rather than any universal realm.

From issues surrounding technology and its implications for the nature of humanity to questions of race and gender, *The Phantom Menace* offers evidence of some of the questions that trouble – or are evaded by – late twentieth-century Western society. As suggested in the introduction, however, these thematic and sub-textual elements can never be entirely divorced from factors relating to the more prosaic industrial domain. Many elements of the film can be explained quite fully in these terms alone. Ultimately, what is required is a blend of these different levels of analysis, something we hope to have demonstrated throughout this book.

GLOSSARY

Definitions given here are related to the specific use made of these terms in their place of appearance in the text.

atonal music
Music that is not based on conventional major or minor scales; atonal music tends to have an elusive or unsettling effect.

Bauhaus
An influential style developed in Germany in the early-twentieth century; it sought simplicity and functionality through a lack of ornamentation, with the aim of bringing art and technology together through the use of chrome-plated tubing in furniture, glass and concrete in buildings; Bauhaus became one of the key looks of 'modernism' and is frequently used in corporate offices.

blue or green screen
Background screens against which live-action elements are filmed, later to be combined with special effects footage.

chaos theory
An approach based on the idea that small changes in conditions at one stage can bring about sudden or unexpectedly large shifts elsewhere; most commonly explained, as in *Jurassic Park*, through the allegorical example of the 'butterfly effect', according to which the spread of a butterfly's wing in one location might affect patterns of air movement that eventually create major weather effects in another part of the world.

computer-generated effects
Special effects created in computers by transforming images into digital information that can be manipulated freely.

continuity editing
A system used to ensure that characters, objects and backgrounds maintain a consistent sense of spatial organisation when presented through numerous shots taken from different positions.

cultural capital
A term used to describe how social inequalities extend into the consumption of cultural products; taste, competencies and values are dependent on our place in the social hierarchy, including access to resources such as education and leisure time.

cyberpunk
Initially a description of the writing of William Gibson in the early 1980s; now used more widely to define a sub-genre characterised by subcultural uses of computers and other types of technology, such as neuro-implants, which permit physical interaction with the digital world.

cyborg
A hybrid mix of organic, computer and mechanical parts.

diegetic music
Produced by people or objects within the fictional world created by a film.

dystopian
The antithesis of utopian; figuring a nightmarish world in which rational impulses to engineer society back-fire dangerously.

expressionist
A style in which internal psychological states are projected through striking angular and asymmetrical designs onto the external landscape; developed in the German visual arts and theatre in the early twentieth century and especially associated in film with the works of German film-makers in the 1920s.

fractal
The generation of complexity from simple origins.

futurist
A utopian art movement founded in Italy by Filippo Tommaso Marinetti's *Futurist Manifesto* of 1909; it sought to produce art for the machine age celebrating speed, dynamism and the fusion of the body and technology.

gaze
A term referring to the exchange of looks that takes place in the cinema; widely discussed by psychoanalytic film theorists, in particular Laura Mulvey, who argued that the female is predominantly the object of the male gaze.

genre
From the French for 'kind' or 'type'. Used in a cinematic context to categorise or typify films in a variety of different ways.

gothic
A term used in the eighteenth century to describe that which diverged from the principles of Enlightenment and classicism; associated with an atmosphere of mystery, supernatural terrors, decorative or other types of excess and ornamentation – and the evocation of the archaic and the irrational.

historical determinism
The argument that our fate is determined by the broad movement of history, beyond individual control.

ideology
A word that has been used in many different ways; here, meaning a dominant – although not always coherent – system of ideas or understandings of the world.

immersion
A process in which we do not just sit back at a distance but are taken physically into the space of the fiction in one way or another.

interactivity
A process in which we can directly affect the fictional world ourselves, rather than remaining a passive recipient of the experience.

intertextual links
References to other texts; made intentionally by film-makers or through associations brought by the viewer.

Manga
Japanese animated features based upon a series of comics.

Mandelbrot set
A computer generated image produced by a mathematical equation developed by Benoit Mandelbrot; based on fractal geometry, it repeats the same shapes infinitely at different scales.

New Hollywood
A term that has been used with different emphasis by different commentators, but that generally means the Hollywood that followed the collapse of the vertically- integrated studio system during the 1950s; once used primarily in connection with the work of a new generation of film-makers who came to the fore in the late 1960s and early 1970s, it is now often used to signify the domination of the industry by companies located within larger entertainment conglomerates.

non-diegetic music
Music not directly produced by anyone or anything in the fictional space of the film; most film music is non-diegetic.

non-pitched synthesised sound
Electronically produced sound occupying the ground between sound effects and music.

pastiche
Works of art or culture that copy others without irony or intending to be passed off as the originals; a concept central to the theory of postmodernism developed by Fredric Jameson.

political correctness
A term often used to ridicule or oppose supposedly 'excessive' attempts to stamp out the likes of sexism and racism; often used as a cover for a backlash against such moves.

pre-sold
A term used to refer to products that have already established an identity in the marketplace, rather than being original new works.

product placement
The use of films as shop windows for advertising products.

psychoanalysis
A methodology derived from the writings of Sigmund Freud and Jacques Lacan on the formation of the psyche; concepts such as the unconscious, repression and desire are used to analyse films and the pleasures they offer spectators.

queer
Queer theory takes up the position of the 'unnatural', using it to subvert and expose dominant cultural practices, particularly in terms of sexuality and gender.

rationality
A mode of explaining the world that is grounded in reason and objectivity rather than emotion and subjectivity.

schizophrenia
Medically, a condition defined as a psychosis in which the sufferer is cut off from the world and unable to distinguish fantasy from reality; a concept taken up by Jameson from the psychoanalytic theory of Jacques Lacan (and used in a more liberationist sense by Gilles Deleuze and Felix Guattari).

science
Knowledge gained by systematic observation.

semantic
Relating to meaning, especially the meaning of words.

structuralist
An approach based on teasing out the structures of oppositions found underlying cultural products.

surrealism
An early twentieth-century art movement heavily influenced by psychoanalysis, surrealism set out to explore the irrational world of the subconscious and tended to produce bizarre images

through anomalous meetings of diverse concepts, such as those exemplified by Salvador Dali's 'soft watches'.

syntactic
Relating to grammatical structure.

technology
Applied science, prosthetic devices and products used to extend the sphere of human operation: hand-axe, computer or vacuum cleaner.

texture mapping
The process in which digitally produced texture is applied to the 'skin' overlaid on the wire-frame of basic shapes in certain types of computer animation.

trope
Literally a 'figure or turn of speech'; often used in the study of cultural products to mean a stylistic or rhetorical device that may be specific to a genre or individual film.

utopian
An imaginary state of ideal harmony and perfection derived from Thomas More's *Utopia* (1516).

vertically integrated
A system in which the same company controls different levels of a business; in this case the production, distribution and exhibition of films.

virtual reality
Computer simulations of perceptual fields in three dimensions.

FILMOGRAPHY

Note: Different sources often give differing dates for the same film, a confusion arising from the fact that some use the date of production, while others give the year of release in one country or another. For the sake of consistency we have used a single source, the Internet Movie DataBase (www.us.imdb.com), which uses the date of release, usually in the United States.

π (Darren Aronofsky, 1998, US)
2001: A Space Odyssey (Stanley Kubrick, 1968, US/UK)
A Connecticut Yankee in King Arthur's Court (Tay Garnett, 1949, US)
Alien (Ridley Scott, 1979, UK)
Alien 3 (David Fincher, 1992, US)
Alien Nation (Graham Baker, 1988, US)
Alien Resurrection (Jean-Pierre Jeunet, 1997, US)
Aliens (James Cameron, 1986, US)
Alphaville (Jean-Luc Godard, 1965, Fr./It.)
Amazing Colossal Man, The (Bert I. Gordon, 1957, US)
Apollo 13 (Ron Howard, 1995, US)
Armageddon (Michael Bay, 1998, US)
Arrival, The (David Twohy, 1996, US)
Attack of the 50ft Woman (Nathan Hertz/Juran, 1957, US)
Attack of the 50ft Woman (Christopher Guest, 1993, US)
Attack of the Crab Monsters (Roger Corman, 1956, US)
Attack of the Killer Tomatoes (John De Bello, 1978, US)
Back to the Future (Robert Zemeckis, 1985, US)
Back to the Future Part II (Robert Zemeckis, 1989, US)
Back to the Future Part III (Robert Zemeckis, 1990, US)
Barbarella (Roger Vadim, 1968, Fr./It.)
Birth of a Nation, The (D. W. Griffith, 1915, US)

Blade Runner (Ridley Scott, 1982, US)
Born in Flames (Lizzie Borden, 1983, US)
Brain Eaters, The (Bruno VeSota, 1958, US)
Brainstorm (Douglas Trumbull, 1983, US)
Brazil (Terry Gilliam, 1985, UK)
Bride of Frankenstein (James Whale, 1935, US)
Brother From Another Planet, The (John Sayles, 1984, US)
City of Lost Children, The (Marc Caro, Jean-Pierre Jeunet, 1995, Fr.)
Close Encounters of the Third Kind (Steven Spielberg, 1977, US)
Cocoon (Ron Howard, 1985, US)
Contact (Robert Zemeckis, 1997, US)
Coppélia ou la Poupée Animée (Georges Méliès, 1900, Fr.)
Creature from the Black Lagoon (Jack Arnold, 1954, US)
Cube (Vincenzo Natali, 1997, Can.)
Dark City (Alex Proyas, 1997, US)
Dark Star (John Carpenter, 1973, US)
Day the Earth Stood Still, The (Robert Wise, 1951, US)
Deep Blue Sea (Renny Harlin, 1999, US)
Deep Impact (Mimi Leder, 1998, US)
Demolition Man (Marco Brambilla, 1993, US)
Demon Seed (Donald Cammell, 1977, US)
Destination Moon (Irving Pichel, 1950, US)
Devil Girl From Mars (David MacDonald, 1954, UK)
Dr Who and the Daleks (Gordon Flemyng, 1965, UK)
Dr Jekyll and Mr Hyde (Rouben Mamoulian, 1931, US)
Dune (David Lynch, 1984, US)
E.T. The Extra-Terrestrial (Steven Spielberg, 1982, US)
Earth vs. the Flying Saucers (Fred F. Sears, 1956, US)
Event Horizon (Paul Anderson, 1997, US)
eXistenZ (David Cronenberg, 1999, Can./UK)
Fantastic Voyage (Richard Fleischer, 1966, US)
Fifth Element, The (Luc Besson, 1997, Fr./US)
Flesh Gordon (Michael Benvensite, Howard Ziehm, 1972, US)
Flight to Mars (Leslie Selander, 1951, US)
Fly, The (David Cronenberg, 1986, US)
Forbidden Planet (Fred M. Wilcox, 1956, US)
Frankenstein (James Whale, 1931, US)
Gattaca (Andrew Niccol, 1997, US)
Godzilla (Roland Emmerich, 1998, US)
Gojira aka *Godzilla King of Monsters* (Ishiro Honda, 1954, Jap./US)
Gone with the Wind (Victor Fleming, 1939, US)
Gugusse et l'Automate (Georges Méliès, 1897, Fr.)
Hackers (Iain Softley, 1995, US)

Handmaid's Tale, The (Volker Schlöndorff, 1990, US/Ger.)

Hardware (Richard Stanley, 1990, UK)

Honey, I Shrunk the Kids (Joe Johnston, 1989, US)

I Married a Monster from Outer Space (Gene Fowler Jr, 1958, US)

Incredible Shrinking Man, The (Jack Arnold, 1957, US)

Incredible Shrinking Woman, The (Joel Schumacher, 1981, US)

Independence Day (Roland Emmerich, 1996, US)

InnerSpace (Joe Dante, 1987, US)

Invaders from Mars (William Cameron Menzies, 1953, US)

Invasion of the Body Snatchers (Don Siegel, 1956, US)

Invasion of the Body Snatchers (Philip Kaufman, 1978, US)

Invasion of the Saucer Men (Edward L. Cahn, 1957, US)

Invisible Boy, The (Herman Hoffman, 1957, US)

Invisible Man, The (James Whale, 1933, US)

It Came From Outer Space (Jack Arnold, 1953, US)

It Conquered the World (Roger Corman, 1956, US)

Johnny Mnemonic (Robert Longo, 1995, Can.)

Judge Dredd (Danny Cannon, 1995, US)

Jurassic Park (Steven Spielberg, 1993, US)

La Jetée (Chris Marker, 1963, Fr.)

Last Starfighter, The (Nick Castle, 1984, US)

Lawnmower Man, The (Brett Leonard, 1992, UK/US)

Lethal Weapon (Richard Donner, 1987, US)

Le Voyage dans la Lune (Georges Méliès, 1902, Fr.)

Logan's Run (Michael Anderson, 1976, US)

Lost in Space (Stephen Hopkins, 1998, US/UK)

Mad Love (Karl Freund, 1935, US)

Mad Max (George Miller, 1979, Aus.)

Mad Max 2 (George Miller, 1981, Aus.)

Mad Max Beyond Thunderdome (George Miller, 1985, Aus./UK)

Mars Attacks! (Tim Burton, 1996, US)

Matrix, The (Andy Wachowski, Larry Wachowski, 1999, US)

Men in Black (Barry Sonnenfeld, 1997, US)

Metropolis (Fritz Lang, 1927, Ger.)

Mimic (Guillermo del Toro, 1997, US)

Mysterious Island, The (Lucien Hubbard, 1929, US)

Navigator: A Medieval Odyssey, The (Vincent Ward, 1988, NZ)

Night of the Lepus (William F. Claxton, 1972, US)

Plan 9 From Outer Space (Edward D. Wood, 1958, US)

Planet of the Apes (Franklin J. Schaffner, 1968, US)

Planet of the Vampires (Mario Bava, 1965, It./Sp.)

Quatermass and the Pit (Roy Ward Baker, 1967, UK)

Quatermasss Xperiment, The (Val Guest, 1955, UK)

Queen of Outer Space (Edward Bernds, 1958, US)
Repo Man (Alex Cox, 1984, US)
Return of the Jedi (Richard Marquand, 1983, US)
Right Stuff, The (Philip Kaufman, 1983, US)
RoboCop (Paul Verhoeven, 1987, US)
Rocketship X-M (Kurt Neumann, 1950)
Scanners (David Cronenberg, 1980, Can.)
Short Circuit (John Badham, 1986, US)
Silent Running (Douglas Trumbull, 1971, US)
Sleeper (Woody Allen, 1973, US)
Solaris (Andrei Tarkovsky, 1972, USSR)
Soylent Green (Richard Fleischer, 1973, US)
Spawn (Mark Dippé, 1997, US)
Sphere (Barry Levinson, 1998, US)
Star Trek: First Contact (Jonathan Frakes, 1996, US)
Star Wars (George Lucas, 1977, US)
Star Wars: Episode One – The Phantom Menace (George Lucas, 1999, US)
Stargate (Roland Emmerich, 1994, US)
Starship Troopers (Paul Verhoeven, 1997, US)
Stepford Wives, The (Bryan Forbes, 1975, US)
Strange Days (Kathryn Bigelow, 1995, US)
Tank Girl (Rachel Talalay, 1995, US)
Terminator, The (James Cameron, 1984, US)
Terminator 2: Judgment Day (James Cameron, 1991, US)
Testament of Dr Mabuse, The (Fritz Lang, 1933, Ger.)
Thing, The (aka *The Thing (From Another World)*) (Christopher Nyby, 1951, US)
Them! (Gordon Douglas, 1954, US)
Things to Come (William Cameron Menzies, 1936, UK)
This Island Earth (Joseph Newman, 1954, US)
THX 1138 (George Lucas, 1970, US)
Time Machine, The (George Pal, 1960, US)
Titanic (James Cameron, 1997, US)
Tron (Steven Lisberger, 1982, US)
Twelve Monkeys (Terry Gilliam, 1995, US)
Videodrome (David Cronenberg, 1982, Can./US)
Village of the Damned (Wolf Rilla, 1960, UK)
Virtuosity (Brett Leonard, 1995, US)
Voodoo Woman (Edward L. Cahn, 1957, US)
War of the Worlds (Byron Haskins, 1953, US)
Wargames (John Badham, 1983, US)
Waterworld (Kevin Reynolds, 1995, US)
Westworld (Michael Crichton, 1973, US)
X-Men (Bryan Singer, 2000, US)

X Files Movie, The (Rob Bowman, 1998, US/Can.)
Zardoz (John Boorman, 1973, UK)

Television Series

Babylon 5 (1994–1995, US)
Buck Rogers (1940, US)
Buffy The Vampire Slayer (1997–present, US)
Dr Who (1963–1989, UK)
Flash Gordon (1936, US)
I Dream of Jeannie (1965–1970, US)
Lost in Space (1965–1968, US)
Star Trek (1966–1969, US)
Star Trek: The Next Generation (1987–1994, US)
Thunderbirds (1963–1967, UK)
The X Files (1993–present, US)

BIBLIOGRAPHY

The bibliography lists works cited in the text and is also designed to point to useful further reading. The annotated list of 'essential reading' highlights works considered to be of particular importance to contemporary understandings of science fiction cinema, although many valuable contributions are also to be found under 'secondary reading'.

ESSENTIAL READING

Altman, Rick (1984) 'A Semantic/Syntactic Approach to Film Genre', *Cinema Journal* 23, 3, 6–18.
> Outlines a clear and useful conceptual starting point for genre theory, although one that Altman has himself qualified to some extent in later work (see below).

Baudrillard, Jean (1994) *Simulations and Simulacra*. Michigan: University of Michigan Press.
> Recently used in The Matrix as an 'in-joke', this book was intended as a warning against the perils of postmodern culture but has become something of a bible in cyber-culture. Its often second-hand echoes sound in many recent science fiction films.

Bukatman, Scott (1993) *Terminal Identity: The Virtual Subject in Postmodern Science Fiction*. Durham and London: Duke University Press.
> Drawing on a diverse range of films, literature, games and GUIs to map the territory of postmodern culture, Bukatman provides a detailed and theoretical study of the interface between technology and humanity, of use to those readers seeking an analysis of the meaning of cyberculture.

Featherstone, Mike and Roger Burrows (eds) (1995) *Cyberspace/Cyberbodies/Cyberpunk*. London: Sage.
> Collection of essays covering a range of contemporary critical theory and locating science fiction cinema since the mid-1980s within a broader context of digital technologies. Covers issues that have come to the fore in the study of contemporary culture, including gender, the body, virtual reality and cyborgs.

Haraway, Donna (1985) 'A Manifesto for Cyborgs: Science, Technology and Socialist Feminism in the 1980s', *Socialist Review*, 15, 80, 65–107.

An influential and much-cited vision of a 'post-gender' version of the technologically endowed body to which many writings on cyber-embodiment and 'post-humanism' are indebted.

Hardy, Phil (ed.) (1995) *The Aurum Film Encyclopaedia: Science Fiction*. London: Aurum Press.

Provides brief plot outlines and significant features of science fiction films from the late 19th century to the mid-1980s. A useful first-stop resource for those seeking a general sense of the breadth of the genre.

Jancovich, Mark (1996) *Rational Fears: American Horror in the 1950s*. Manchester and New York: Manchester University Press.

A valuable account of American horror, science fiction cinema and literature in the 1950s, placing emphasis on the social and political context of the decade. Jancovich provides a useful overview of the problems of genre criticism, arguing that 1950s American popular films are more than simply the 'invasion' narratives for which they have often been taken.

Kuhn, Annette (ed.) (1990) *Alien Zone: Cultural Theory and Contemporary Science Fiction Cinema*. London: Verso.

This collection provides some impressive essays on films such as Alien, Blade Runner and The Terminator that have been key to recent science fiction studies. Includes contributions from many authors who have proved influential in the critical appraisal of the genre.

—— (ed.) (1999) *Alien Zone II: The Spaces of Science Fiction Cinema*. London: Verso.

Another useful collection in this sequel that explores spaces ranging from those of the futuristic city to cyberspace and the body.

Landon, Brooks (1992) *The Aesthetics of Ambivalence: Rethinking the Science Fiction Film in the Age of Electronic (Re)production*. Westport and London: Greenwood Press.

A stimulating account which gives an important role to the often neglected place of special effects in science fiction. Suggests that computer and other media technologies have led science fiction to overflow its traditional genre boundaries.

Sobchack, Vivian (1993) *Screening Space: The American Science Fiction Film*. New York: Ungar.

One of the first serious full-length studies of the genre, first published in 1980. Originally a traditional genre study, supplemented in the second edition by a new chapter highly influenced by theories of postmodernism.

SECONDARY READING

Altman, Rick (1999) *Film/Genre*. London: BFI Publishing.

Asimov, Isaac (1971) *I, Robot*. London: Voyager. First published 1950.

Balio, Tino (1990) *Hollywood in the Age of Television*. Boston and London: Unwin Hyman.

Barker, Martin and Kate Brooks (1998) *Knowing Audiences: Judge Dredd, Its Friends, Fans and Foes*. Luton: University of Luton Press.

Benshoff, Harry M. (1997) *Monsters in the Closet: Homosexuality and the Horror Film*. Manchester and New York: Manchester University Press.

Biskind, Peter (1983) *Seeing is Believing: How Hollywood Taught Us to Stop Worrying and Love the Fifties*. New York: Pantheon Books.

—— (1998) *Easy Riders, Raging Bulls*. London: Bloomsbury.

Bogle, Donald (1993) *Toms, Coons, Mulattoes, Mammies, and Bucks: An Interpretive History of Blacks in American Films*. New York: Continuum.

Bourdieu, Pierre (1986) (trans. Richard Nice) *Distinction: A Social Critique of the Judgement of Taste*. London and New York: Routledge.

Bruno, Giuliana (1990) 'Ramble City: Postmodernism and Blade Runner', in Annette Kuhn (ed.) *Alien Zone: Cultural Theory and Contemporary Science Fiction Cinema*. London: Verso, 61–74.

Campbell, Joseph (1949) *The Hero with a Thousand Faces*. Princeton NJ: Princeton University Press.

Clover, Carol (1992) *Men, Women and Chainsaws: Gender in the Modern Horror Film*. London: BFI.

Cole, Cheryl (2000) 'Making money from the toy story', *Investors Week*, 31 March, 24–5.

Creed, Barbara (1993) *The Monstrous Feminine: Film, Feminism, Psychoanalysis*. London and New York: Routledge.

Dean, Jodi (1988) *Aliens in America: Conspiracy Cultures from Outerspace to Cyberspace*. Ithaca and London: Cornell University Press.

Earnest, Olen J. (1985) '*Star Wars*: A Case Study of Motion Picture Marketing', in Current Research in Film, 1.

Gray, Charles Hables, Heidi J. Figueroa-Sarriera and Steven Mentor (eds) (1995) *The Cyborg Handbook*. London and New York: Routledge.

Halberstam, Judith and Ira Livingstone (eds) (1995) *Posthuman Bodies*. Bloomington and Indianapolis: Indiana University Press.

Hill, John and Pamela Church Gibson (eds) (1998) *The Oxford Guide to Film Studies*. Oxford and New York: Oxford University Press.

Hillier, Jim (1993) *The New Hollywood*. London: Studio Vista.

James, Edward (1994) *Science Fiction in the 20th Century*. Oxford and New York: Oxford University Press.

Jameson, Fredric (1985) 'Postmodernism and Consumer Society', in Hal Foster (ed.) *Postmodern Culture*. London and Sydney: Pluto Press, 111–25.

—— (1991) *Postmodernism: or, The Cultural Logic of Late Capitalism*. London and New York: Verso.

Kaplan, David A. (1999) 'How George Lucas orchestrated the biggest movie-marketing campaign of all time and made *Phantom* a must-see, no matter what the critics say', *Newsweek*, 17 May 1999, 64–8.

King, Geoff (1999) 'The Scientist as Pioneer Hero: Hollywood's Mythological Reconciliations in Twister and Contact', *Science as Culture*, 8, 3, 371–9.

Kramer, Peter (1998) 'Women First: 'Titanic' action-adventure films and Hollywood's female audience', *Historical Journal of Film, Radio and Television*, 18, 4, 599–618.

Krzywinska, Tanya (2000) *A Skin for Dancing In: Possession, Witchcraft and Voodoo in Film*. Trowbridge: Flicks Books.

Landow, George P. (1992) *Hypertext: The Convergence of Contemporary Critical Theory and Technology*. Baltimore and London: Johns Hopkins University Press.

Landsberg, Alison (1995) 'Prosthetic Memory: *Total Recall* and *Blade Runner*' in Featherstone and Burrows (eds) (1995) *Cyberspace/Cyberbodies/Cyberpunk*. London: Sage, 175–89.

La Valley, Albert (1985) 'Traditions of Trickery: The Role of Special Effects in the Science Fiction Film', in G. E. Slusser and E. S. Rabkin (eds) *Shadows of the Magic Lamp*. Carbondale: Southern Illinois University Press, 141–58.

Lavery, David, Angela Hague and Maria Cartwright (1996) *Deny All Knowledge: Reading The X-Files*. London: Faber.

Levi-Strauss, Claude (1968) *Structural Anthropology*. Harmondsworth: Penguin.

Locanio, P. (1987) *Them or Us: Archetypal Interpretations of Fifties Alien Invasion Narratives*. Bloomington: Indiana University Press.

Lukk, Tiiu (1997) *Movie Marketing: Opening the Picture and Giving it Legs*. Los Angeles: Silman-James Press.

Lyotard, Jean-Francois (1984) *The Postmodern Condition: A Report on Knowledge*. Manchester: Manchester University Press.

Mandelbrot, Benoit (1982) *The Fractal Geometry of Nature*. New York: Freeman.

Metz, Christian (1977) 'Trucage and the Film', in *Critical Enquiry*, 13, 4, 657–75.

Motion Picture Association of America (2000) *1999 Economic Review*. Available on-line at http://www.mpaa.org/useconomicreview/1999Economic

Murray, Janet (1997) *Hamlet on the Holodeck: The Future of Narrative in Cyberspace*. Cambridge, Massachussets: MIT Press.

Mulvey, Laura (1975) 'Visual Pleasure and Narrative Cinema', *Screen*, 16,3, Autumn 1975, 6–18.

Neale, Steve (1990) '"You've Got To Be Fucking Kidding!" Knowledge, Belief and Judgement in Science Fiction', in Annette Kuhn (ed.) *Alien Zone: Cultural Theory and Contemporary Science Fiction Cinema*. London: Verso, 160–8.

—— (2000) *Genre and Hollywood*. London and New York: Routledge.

Newton, Judith (1990) 'Feminism and Anxiety in *Alien*' in Annette Kuhn (ed.) *Alien Zone: Cultural Theory and Contemporary Science Fiction Cinema*. London: Verso, 82–7.

Penley, Constance (1990) 'Time Travel, Primal Scene and Critical Dystopia' in Annette Kuhn (ed.) *Alien Zone: Cultural and Contemporary Science Fiction Cinema*. London: Verso, 116–27.

—— (1997) *NASA/Trek: Popular Science and Sex in America*. Verso: London.

Penley, Constance, Elisabeth Lyon and Lynn Spigel (eds) (1991) *Close Encounters: Film, Feminism and Science Fiction*. Minneapolis and London: University of Minnesota Press.

Pierson, Michele (1999) 'CGI Effects in Hollywood Science Fiction Cinema 1989–95: The Wonder Years', in *Screen* 40, 2, 158–77.

Rux, Brian (1996) *Architects of the Underworld: Unriddling Atlantis, Anomalies of Mars, and the Mystery of the Sphinx*. Berkeley: Frog.

—— (1997) *Hollywood vs. the Aliens*. Berkeley: Frog.

Ryan, Michael and Douglas Kellner (1988) *Camera Politica: The Politics and Ideology of Contemporary Hollywood Film*. Bloomington: Indiana University Press.

Sammon, Paul (1996) *Future Noir: The Making of Blade Runner*. London: Orion.

Schatz, Thomas (1981) *Hollywood Genres: Formulas, Filmmaking, and the Studio System*. New York: McGraw-Hill.

Schelde, Per (1993) *Androids, Humanoids and Other Science Fiction Monsters: Science and Soul in Science Fiction Films*. New York: NYU Press.

Slusser, George E. and Erik S. Rabkin (eds) *Shadows of the Magic Lamp*. Carbondale: Southern Illinois University Press.

Smith, Thomas G. (1991) *Industrial Light and Magic: The Art of Special Effects*. London: Virgin.

Soja, Edward (1989) *Postmodern Geographies: The Reassertion of Space in Critical Social Theory*. London and New York: Verso.

Sontag, Susan (1966) 'The Imagination of Disaster', in *Against Interpretation and Other Essays*. New York: Farrar, Straus and Giroux, 209–25.

Tasker, Yvonne (1993) *Spectacular Bodies: Gender, Genre and the Action Cinema*. London and New York: Routledge.

Telotte, J.P. (1995) *Replications: A Robotic History of the Science Fiction Film*. Urbana: University of Illinois.

—— (1999) *A Distant Technology: Science Fiction Film and the Machine Age*. Hanover: Wesleyan University Press.

Thomson, David (1998) *The Alien Quartet*. London: Bloomsbury.

Tudor, Andrew (1989) *Monsters and Mad Scientists: A Cultural History of the Horror Movie*. Oxford: Blackwell.

Vaz, Mark Cotta and Patricia Rose Duignan (1996) *Industrial Light and Magic: Into the Digital Realm*. London: Virgin.

Wasko, Janet (1994) *Hollywood in the Information Age: Beyond the Silver Screen*. Cambridge: Polity Press.

WAR CINEMA
Hollywood on the Front Line
Guy Westwell

'This compact text succinctly summarises the current scholarship and suggests future projects for interested readers to follow.'
– Peter C. Rollins,
Editor-in-Chief, *Film & History*

£12.99 pbk
1-904764-54-1

DOCUMENTARY
The Margins of Reality
Paul Ward

'This book speaks in a lucid way to a number of the most important issues in documentary film studies at the beginning of the twenty-first century.'
– Prof. Brian Winston,
University of Lincoln

£12.99 pbk
1-904764-59-2

ITALIAN NEOREALISM
Rebuilding the Cinematic City
Mark Shiel

'The discussions of the films in question are always based upon very intelligent and sensitive analyses. Highly recommended.'
– Peter Bondanella,
Indiana University

£12.99 pbk
1-904764-48-7

TEEN MOVIES
American Youth on Screen
Timothy Shary

'A much-needed primer on the teen film: a linear, concise yet comprehensive study of one of modern American cinema's most popular genres.'
– Jon Lewis,
Oregon State University

£12.99 pbk
1-904764-49-5

THE NEW HOLLYWOOD
From Bonnie and Clyde to Star Wars
Peter Krämer

'Rigorous, thorough and lucid, this book ... invites us to reconsider this particular era in Hollywood's history and the approach to the study of its films.'
– Steve Neale,
University of Exeter

£12.99 pbk
1-904764-58-4

FILM NOIR
From Berlin to Sin City
Mark Bould

'A wonderfully compact and engaging entrée to the dark, doomed world of film noir ... this book is an indispensable addition to the growing literature on this most vital and compelling of film genres'
– Bob Miklitsch,
Ohio University

£12.99 pbk
1-904764-50-9

FILM PERFORMANCE
From Achievement
to Appreciation
Andrew Klevan

£12.99 pbk
1-904764-24-X

'A first-rate work ... highly
original in its approach,
beautifully written, and
elegantly crafted to make its
strong case without wasting
a word.'
– William Rothman,
University of Miami

THE MUSICAL
Race, Gender
and Performance
Susan Smith

£12.99 pbk
1-904764-37-1

'A theoretically informed
and lively, elegantly written
volume that will appeal to
all students of the formal
and social meanings of the
musical.'
– Peter Evans, Queen Mary,
University of London

NEW DIGITAL
CINEMA
Reinventing
the Moving Image
Holly Willis

£12.99 pbk
1-904764-25-8

'This book delivers a highly
readable and much needed
survey of the diverse currents
coursing through the circuits
of digital cinema.'
– Chris Darke, author of
*Light Readings: Film Criticism
and Screen Arts*

FEMINIST FILM
STUDIES
Writing the Woman
into Cinema
Janet McCabe

£12.99 pbk
1-904764-03-7

'This readable history of
the intellectual evolution of
feminist film studies emerges
after real "road-testing" in
the classroom.'
– Diane Negra, University
of East Anglia

MELODRAMA
Genre, Style, Sensibility
John Mercer
and Martin Shingler

£12.99 pbk
1-904764-02-9

'An excellent introduction
... it expands understanding
of key concepts related to
genre, aesthetics, ideology
and problems of reading and
response.'
– Christine Gledhill,
Staffordshire University

MUSIC IN FILM
Soundtracks and Synergy
Pauline Reay

£12.99 pbk
1-903364-65-5

'A thorough overview of
the major developments in
mainstream film music, this
introduction develops into a
welcome and much-needed
focus on the pop score and
soundtrack with excellent
and original choices of case
study films and performers.'
– David Butler, University
of Manchester

EARLY CINEMA
From Factory Gate
to Dream Factory
Simon Popple
and Joe Kember

£12.99 pbk
1-903364-58-2

'Bringing new perspectives
and rigour to the study of film
and popular culture, there is
a real need for the up-to-date
introduction that Popple and
Kember provide.'
– Ian Christie, Birkbeck
College, University of London

BRITISH SOCIAL REALISM
From Documentary
to Brit Grit
Samantha Lay

£12.99 pbk
1-903364-41-8

'A long-overdue introduction
... it fills an important gap in
the literature and will be of
considerable interest any-
where that courses on British
cinema are offered.'
– Steve Chibnall, De Montfort
University

NEW GERMAN CINEMA
Images of a Generation
Julia Knight

£12.99 pbk
1-903364-28-0

'Delineates and explains
with welcome lucidity how
historically specific conditions made possible the birth
of the New German Cinema in
the 1960s and brought about
its demise.'
– Klaus Phillips,
Hollins University

WOMEN'S CINEMA
The Contested Screen
Alison Butler

£12.99 pbk
1-903364-27-2

'An invaluable addition to
the literature, offering new
and valuable material while
clarifying vexed, overly-
debated issues once and for
all ... beautifully written.'
– Pamela Church Gibson,
The London Institute

PRODUCTION DESIGN
Architects of the Screen
Jane Barnwell

£12.99 pbk
1-903364-55-8

'This book is more comprehensive than anything before
– masses of research and
opinion analysed with real
insight and understanding.'
– Stuart Craig,
production designer

FILM EDITING
The Art of the Expressive
Valerie Orpen

£12.99 pbk
1-903364-53-1

'An exceptionally intelligent
book about a notoriously
elusive subject: editing in
various kinds and modes of
narrative filmmaking.'
– Brian Henderson,
University of Buffalo, SUNY

ANIMATION
Genre and Authorship
Paul Wells

'Absolutely excellent. It clearly introduces areas which do not have an adequate literature ... succinct and precise enough to be used as a starting point for students' research.'
– David Huxley, Manchester Metropolitan University

£12.99 pbk
1-903364-20-5

SCENARIO
The Craft of Screenwriting
Tudor Gates

'This is an immensely readable introduction to the craft of screenwriting and is very helpful for budding screenwriters.'
– Alby James, Northern Film School, Leeds Metropolitan University

£12.99 pbk
1-903364-26-4

NEW CHINESE CINEMA
Challenging Representations
Sheila Cornelius
with Ian Haydn Smith

'Very thorough in its coverage ... clearly written and appropriately targeted at an undergraduate audience.'
– Leon Hunt, Brunel University

£12.99 pbk
1-903364-13-2

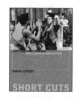

COSTUME AND CINEMA
Dress Codes in Popular Film
Sarah Street

'A valuable addition to the growing literature on film and costume ... engagingly written, offering a lucid introduction to the field.'
– Stella Bruzzi, Royal Holloway, University of London

£12.99 pbk
1-903364-18-3

MISE-EN-SCÈNE
Film Style and Interpretation
John Gibbs

'The book is an excellent introduction not just to *mise-en-scène* but to the study of film in general, as well as a reminder of what serious film criticism should be about.'
– *Film and Film Culture*

£12.99 pbk
1-903364-06-X

PSYCHOANALYSIS AND CINEMA
The Play of Shadows
Vicky Lebeau

'A very lucid and subtle exploration of the reception of Freud's theories and their relation to psychoanalysis' contemporary developments – cinema and modernism.'
– Elizabeth Cowie, University of Kent

£12.99 pbk
1-903364-19-1

THE WESTERN GENRE
From Lordsburg
to Big Whiskey
John Saunders

'A clear exposition of the
major thematic currents of
the genre providing attentive
and illuminating reading of
major examples.'
– Ed Buscombe, editor of
the *BFI Companion to the
Western*

£12.99 pbk
1-903364-12-4

DISASTER MOVIES
The Cinema of
Catastrophe
(second edition)
Stephen Keane

'A lively and engaging
account of the mayhem
inflicted on the world by
Hollywood'
– Geoff King, University
of Brunel

£12.99 pbk
1-905674-03-1

READING
HOLLYWOOD
Spaces and Meanings
in American Film
Deborah Thomas

'Amongst the finest intro-
ductions to Hollywood in
particular and film studies
in general ... subtler, more
complex, yet more readable
than most of its rivals, many
of which it will displace.'
– Robin Wood

£12.99 pbk
1-903364-01-9

THE STAR SYSTEM
Hollywood's Production
of Popular Identities
Paul McDonald

'A very good introduction
to the topic filling an existing
gap in the needs of teachers
and students of the subject.'
– Roberta Pearson,
University of Wales, Cardiff

£12.99 pbk
1-903364-02-7

EARLY SOVIET
CINEMA
Innovation, Ideology
and Propaganda
David Gillespie

'An excellent book ... lively
and informative. It fills a
significant gap and deserves
to be on reading lists
wherever courses on Soviet
cinema are run.'
– Graham Roberts,
University of Surrey

£12.99 pbk
1-903364-04-3

THE HORROR GENRE
From Beelzebub
to Blair Witch
Paul Wells

'A valuable contribution to
the body of teaching texts
available ... a book for all
undergraduates starting on
the subject.'
– Linda Ruth Williams,
University of Southampton

£12.99 pbk
1-903364-00-0